ATTITUDE OF GRATITUDE
TRUE WORSHIP

Michael Byrd Ph.D.

Places, events, and situations in this story are purely fictional. The situations have been changed to protect confidentiality. Any resemblance to actual persons, living or dead, is coincidental. All rights reserved. Copyright © 2017 by Michael Byrd. All rights reserved.

No part of this book may be reproduced, stored in a retrieval system, or transmitted by any means, electronic, mechanical, photocopying, recording, or otherwise, without written permission from the author.

ISBN-13: 9780692976043
ISBN-10: 0692976043

TABLE OF CONTENTS

Premise	v
Introduction	ix
Acknowledgements	xi
Attitude of Gratitude	1
Attitude of Gratitude True Worship	3
Patience	8
Patience is Waiting and Trusting in God	9
Manipulation	11
Experience	13
Hopefulness	16
Overcoming Doubts	20
There are Two Kinds of People	24
Sowing and Reaping	26
There is a Purpose Behind our Pain	28
New Identity in Christ	38
Our Lives have a Tendency to go Toward the Direction We Focus	42
Complaining verses Worshiping	48
Blaming	50
Contentment	55

Prophecy, Prediction about Ungrateful People!
Entitlement Mentality 58
Drunk in the Spirit 61
Perceptions 63
Words of Wisdom 66
Are you Poisoning Yourself? 71

Conclusion 73
Appendix 75
Calendar 76

PREMISE

The premise or foundation of this book is based on I Thessalonians 5:18-19, "In everything give thanks: for this is the will of God in Christ Jesus concerning you. 19 Do not quench the Spirit." The heart of true worship is being thankful. This implies that we have a choice to be thankful or not. We can choose to be thankful in every situation. We have to really trust God to be thankful in tough situations. From Romans 8:28, we hear, "and <u>we know all things</u> work together for the good to them that love God to them who are the called according to his purpose. When we <u>know</u> that the bad things we are going through are for our good, we will be thankful; but if we don't know if what we are going through is for our good we will gripe and complain. <u>God wants us to trust Him</u>! We can trust God as Job did. We, too, can trust God so much that we can say, "Though He slay me yet will I trust Him." We could also think like Abraham, who had hope against hope, and have positive expectations when there is only negative expectation. And like David who proclaimed, "Yea, though I walk through the valley of the shadow of death, I will fear no evil: for thou art with me." Finally, we could speak as Jesus spoke to the Father, "not my will but your will be done".

I have learned a rule, principle or law; you may call it, while working with so many inner city youths that some people attract conflict. They attract problems and all types of negative drama. This led me to coin the term "drama magnet!" because they attract negative drama. Drama magnets spread rumors about others. They start up confusion in a school, family, work environment or church. The Bible talks about a law of blessing and cursing. Psalm 109:17 says, "As he loved cursing, so let it come unto him: as he delighted not in blessing, so let it be far from him." Because people curse or talk negative about others, they attract negative to themselves. They attract negative drama! People call them "messy people" because mess seems to follow them. II Peter 3:3 says, "Knowing this first, that there shall come in the last days *scoffers*, walking after their own lusts (God's Word Translation). First, you must understand this: In the last days, people who follow their own desires will appear. These disrespectful people will ridicule God's promise. In these last days, no truer words are spoken. People are disrespectful to one another. They ridicule (or put down) God and God's people.

    I have also seen young people thrive in negative environments. I have seen people that do not get involved in mess even when people keep bringing them mess. Even though people bring them negative talk about others, they don't spread the negative talk to others. They try to say positive things. Because drama magnets love cursing, negative drama comes to the drama magnet. And because drama magnets do not like to bless (or speak well of) others, so blessings were far from them. I've seen people that attract negative things and I have seen people attract positive things. I have learned a lot through the law of blessing and cursing. I try to be like David and proclaim, "I will bless the Lord at all times: his praise shall continually be in my mouth." I make a choice to trust God and be thankful.

    When you are upset about the past, it's called depression. When you are worried about the future, it's called anxiety! But God gives us a gift--the *present*. Enjoy it! Be thankful.

"But thou *art* holy, *O thou* that inhabitest the praises of Israel", Psalm 22:3. Strong's Hebrew Dictionary for Israel states, *"He will rule* as *God. If we allow God to rule our hearts, He will inhabit our praise!" God* dwells in our lives and through our praises. In other words, we become intimate (dwell intimately) with God when we praise God. I believe we are created to have fellowship with God. We are made to worship God! God's greatest desire is to be intimate with His people!

INTRODUCTION

Romans 1:21 tells us, "Because that, when they knew God, they glorified him not as God, neither were thankful; but became vain in their imaginations, and their foolish heart was darkened." Just as the Children of Israel knew God and saw His miracles, they did not glorify Him as God and weren't thankful. We, too, have seen the life changing power of God and have not glorified Him as God. Our hearts have become darkened to the truth in God's word. We need to become more intimate with God. I define praise as glorifying God and worship as becoming intimate with God! True worship comes from a thankful heart. I Thessalonians 5:18-19 we read, "In everything give thanks: for this is the will of God in Christ Jesus concerning you. Do not quench the Spirit." We like the children of Israel complain and become ungrateful. We quench the Spirit; and fall from intimate relationship with God.

My hope is that people will become thankful even during disappointment. They will be able to thank God when God gives something to someone else, even when it is that very thing for which they have been praying. Be thankful to God when others are blessed rather than yourself being blessed. According to I Corinthians 13:4 Amplified Bible (AMP), "Love ... is not jealous *or* envious ..." Jealousy and envy are blessing blockers.

ACKNOWLEDGEMENTS

I like the elders who cast their crowns before the feet of Jesus saying, "Thou art worthy, O Lord, to receive glory and honor and power: for thou hast created all things, and for thy pleasure they are and were created." Revelation 4:11 states, "I haven't done anything without the power of God helping me to achieve it." God is willing to use me to speak to His people even though I ran from the calling to pastor for two decades before accepting the call. I'm forever thankful to God for my wife, Lauretta Byrd, for she is a gift from God. Thanks goes to my spiritual covering, my father in the gospel, Bishop Don V. Nobles of the Texas Lone Star Ecclesiastical Jurisdiction of the Church of God In Christ. Thank you, Gwendolyn Davis, for the hours of work you spent in production. Lastly, deep gratitude goes to my mother, Della Byrd, a living example of Godly living as a woman of God.

ATTITUDE OF GRATITUDE

In Philippians 4:8, Amplified Bible (AMP), it reads, "Finally, believers, whatever is true, whatever is honorable and worthy of respect, whatever is right and confirmed by God's word, whatever is pure and wholesome, whatever is lovely and brings peace, whatever is admirable and of good repute; if there is any excellence, if there is anything worthy of praise, think continually on these things [center your mind on them, and implant them in your heart]." "We can choose to think about good things and be thankful. According to Luke 6:45, King James Version (KJV), what we think and talk about we bring about! When we talk and think about negative things we create negative strongholds of thinking. Every thought creates a neuropathway in the brain. The more we think a thought positive or negative the stronger the neuropathway gets. It is like drawing a straight line against the grain on a piece of wood. Your pen will zigzag because of the wood grain. But once we make a groove in the wood we tend to stay in the groove. The same goes for our thinking. The longer our thinking stays in the groove the harder it becomes to get out of that groove. The more we think negative, the harder it is to get out of that groove of negative thinking. The deeper the groove gets the harder it is to control the thoughts and the thoughts control more and more of the person's life. We have to control our thoughts or our thoughts will control us! In Romans 8:6 New International Version (NIV), "The mind governed by the flesh is death, but the mind governed by the Spirit is life and peace." Worship is expressing our love toward God! The attitude of gratitude, true worship, helps you create a groove of positive thinking! We bring about what we think and talk about!

So I have something for you to do. I want you to create a Gratitude List. It is a powerful way to help you begin a daily practice of being thankful and thus developing a closer relationship with God. I believe this gratitude list can bring you to a place of happiness, regardless of your circumstances. Many people grew up in a negative culture of blaming and complaining. I will talk about blaming and complaining later. The problem is that many of us have been programmed to think about what we don't have and not to be thankful for what we have. The gratitude list can help you notice the wonderful things that you already have in your life. The gratitude list can help you change your vibrational energy to that of a more peaceful person. When we appreciate the little things in life it makes us feel blessed. When you find yourself complaining, if you have a rubber band to put on your wrist, put it on and pop it or use the Attitude of Gratitude wristband. Now turn to the Appendix and read the instructions to begin your Gratitude List on today's date.

ATTITUDE OF GRATITUDE TRUE WORSHIP

When I think about His goodness and all He has done for me my heart cries out hallelujah thank God for saving me! No matter how bad you have it, someone is worse off than you and someone would like to be in your shoes! I don't care how bad things are here in America or in our modern cities, there are people in third world countries that would give anything or do anything to take your place. So be thankful, have an attitude of gratitude and truly worship God, because things could be worse! Creating an attitude takes time. I ask my reader to not only write down things for which they are thankful but to also say out loud the things for which they are grateful. One should also write down any notes about the things for which they are thankful. Speaking to yourself from your gratitude list enables you to renew and transform for Romans 12:2 (NIV) says, "Do not conform to the pattern of this world but be transformed by the renewing of your mind. Then you will be able to test and approve what God's will is—his good, pleasing and perfect will." Renew your mind from this negative world. In other words, reprogram your mind to appreciate what you have, not always focusing on what you don't have! This can help you to enjoy more positive experiences, people, and circumstances.

God began to slowly and gracefully reprogram my prayer time. I would begin to pray for people and situations, and after a few minutes, I would begin to thank God while worshiping before having prayed for the more important things. I began to get mad at myself for not staying focused. Working with so many kids with Attention Deficit Disorder (A.D.D.) caused me to wonder if I was suffering from A.D.D.? I began to ask God what I should do about my inability to focus, for a longer period of time, in my prayer life? I didn't hear an answer. It's funny that I had preached many times from I Thessalonians 5:18, which states, "In everything give thanks, for this is the will of God!" I was thinking the message was for someone else. I would pray about a problem or a painful situation and begin to thank God. Later God showed me that this word Attitude of Gratitude was to help me to help others to trust God in every situation and praise and thank God in every situation. God was transforming me without my knowing it.

As our trust in God grows, our praise and thanks to God will grow as well. As my trust in God grows, I begin to have more and more peace. God wants us to grow up so that we automatically give thanks in everything because it is His will. **2 Thessalonians 1:3 God's Word (GW)** We always have to thank God for you, brothers and sisters. It's right to do this because your faith is showing remarkable growth and your love for each other is increasing. A good example of this is found in Galatians 4:1 (MSG), where it begins, "Let me show you the implications of this: (1) As long as the heir is a minor, he has no advantage over the slave although, legally, he owns the entire inheritance; (2) He is subject to tutors and administrators until whatever date the father has set for emancipation; (3) That is the way it is with us; when we were minors, we were just like slaves ordered around by simple instructions (the tutors and administrators of this world), with no say in the conduct of our own lives; (4) When the time arrived that was set by God the Father, God sent his Son, born among us of a woman, born under the conditions of the law so that he might redeem those of us who have been kidnapped by the law; (5) We have been set free to experience our rightful heritage; (6) You can tell for sure that you are now fully adopted as his own children because God sent the Spirit of his Son into our lives and we cry out, "Papa! Father!" Doesn't that privilege of an intimate conversation with God make it plain that you are not a slave, but a child? And if you are a child, you're also an heir, with complete access to the inheritance. In the natural, if heirs to the throne in any kingdom have a temper tantrum (slave to impulses); that person will not be trusted to conduct the affairs of the kingdom. God wants us to grow up so that we can fulfill Jesus' prayer for God's kingdom to come and for God's will to be done on earth as it is in heaven! God wants us to grow up and change our thinking to that of kings and queens and no longer thinking like slaves. I once was eating dinner with a large church party after a church service. I sat across from a young couple and their one-year old daughter. When the daughter was with her mother they wrestled over the food. When she was in the mother's lap they had a tug of war over a small bowl of fruit. The mother continued to push the bowl away wanting her to grow up and eat one at a time, but the daughter wanted to eat with both hands full of fruits. I also saw her in her father's lap; the father was blowing on her food to cool it. The daughter was not wrestling but was looking patiently at her father as he blew on her food to cool it. She waited patiently for 10 or more blows to cool the food. I first thought she was conditioned to wait by the blowing. But God said to me, "she had learned to trust her father." The father was trying to teach his daughter to blow on it for herself. They both wanted her to grow up so that they could give her more. The mother was pulling the bowl away to keep her from choking on her food. The father wanted to teach his daughter to cool her own food. God wants us to grow to trust Him and wait patiently for Him to give us stuff we are not ready for.

Writing and speaking your gratitude list will help you achieve a positive and appreciative outlook towards your life. More and more days in your life will feel better, your attitude will improve and your reality of this world will mirror more of how God wants this world to be. We will see things as God sees them. The children of Israel that didn't enter into the promised land saw their situation different than Joshua and Caleb saw it in Numbers 13:30-31. Why did Joshua and Caleb see things differently? We know that the children of Israel didn't enter into the Promised Land because they complained. I believe complaining is the polar opposite of trusting God and our faith is activated by what we say and do. Our doubt is also activated by what we say and do. Also, true worship comes from true trust in God. I believe Joshua and Caleb trusted God because they worshiped God. The more you worship the more your trust in God grows. Joshua and Caleb looked at what God had done for them, not at what wasn't done.

Albert Einstein said, "There are only two ways to live your life: One is as though nothing is a miracle; the other is as though everything is a miracle." The people that don't see anything as a miracle seem to take life for granted. The Israelites that didn't get into the Promised Land took God's miracles for granted. After seeing all the miracles God did for them they still did not trust God. They only complained. Paul compares the Israelites in the desert to the early Christians of I Corinthians 10:9-10 New King James (NKJV) ". . . nor let us tempt Christ, as some of them also tempted, and were destroyed by serpents; 10) nor complain, as some of them also complained, and were destroyed by the destroyer." The opposite of trusting God is complaining. Deuteronomy 1:31-32 (AMP) states, "And in the wilderness, where you have seen how the Lord your God bore you, as a man carries his son, in all the way that you went until you came to this place. 32) Yet in spite of this word you did not believe (trust, rely on, and remain steadfast to) the Lord your God. There really are two ways to live your life. One is as though nothing is a miracle. The other is as though everything is a miracle. We should see everything as a miracle and have an Attitude of Gratitude having true worship in our hearts.

There is a growing process. We have to have an Attitude of Gratitude; we have to be thankful. I Thessalonians 5:18 reads, "In everything give thanks; for this is the will of God in Christ Jesus concerning you." People wonder about God's will; is the will of God concerning me in Jesus Christ? God's will is for us to be thankful and to keep an attitude of gratitude or worship! There are important things I want you to focus on to assist you in keeping an attitude of gratitude. Be grateful at all times so that we can give God true worship. Be reminded that when praises go up blessings come down. Just as the children of Israel were thirsty in the desert in Numbers 21:17, "Then Israel sang this song, Spring up, O well; sing ye unto it:" To receive needed water, we, too, need to sing (worship God in) to the thirsty areas of our lives; we can sing to anything we need. We can sing, Money spring up! Transportation spring up! Housing spring up! Psalm 34:9 (MSG) says, "Worship God if you want the best; worship opens doors to all his goodness." God has given to me, the scripture saying in everything give thanks. Be thankful and have an attitude of gratitude; no matter what happens, be thankful. This is God's will in Christ Jesus, no matter what happens, in everything be thankful. In Romans 5:3-5 (KJV), "And not only so, but we glory in tribulations also: knowing that tribulation worketh patience; 4) And patience, experience; and experience, hope: 5) And hope maketh not ashamed; because the love of God is shed abroad in our hearts by the Holy Ghost which is given unto us. This is the growing process. We go from patience, to experience (confidence) to hope (expectation).

PATIENCE

Patience is a virtue! Troubles come to work and develop our patience! We live in a world where we don't have the patience to wait for a package to arrive in its time. We don't want stuff now--we wanted it yesterday! I have seen kids standing in front of a microwave oven yelling hurry up! Come on, what's taking so long! I remember a time when we didn't have microwaves. We had to put the food in the oven and then let time take its place. I believe God wants us to develop patience. David talked a lot about waiting on the Lord. Although he went through troubles, he said, "I will wait on the Lord." I believe David equated waiting with trusting God. I believe God wants us to develop patience and learn to trust Him! I sing a Juanita Bynum song to myself, "I don't mind waiting, I don't mind waiting, I don't mind waiting on the Lord! I don't mind waiting, I don't mind waiting, I don't mind waiting on the Lord!"

PATIENCE IS WAITING AND TRUSTING IN GOD

We can rejoice because we know we are growing in our trust of God. I believe more than anything God wants us to trust Him! One of the most powerful revelations I have received from the Lord is on trusting God! A large part of my job as a crisis interventionist (counselor) in an inner-city school is conducting conflict mediations with students. Over the years of facilitating conflict mediations, I have found that I would rather facilitate one hundred boy conflicts than to facilitate one girl conflict. Girl conflicts are so much harder to resolve! God reminded me of a conflict between two girls that were good friends at one time. The conflict was caused by a rumor about a secret that one girl believed the other had shared. The girl wanted to fight her former friend because she believed her former friend was the person who had shared her secret. She told the story that she had only told two people that secret, and it had to be her (the other girl in mediation) that told it to someone else. The other girl said that she had not shared her secret! It is problematic to appear as if you are taking one person's side over the other during mediation. But I began to push the other girl (sharing her secret) theory. I asked, "Could it be that the other girl shared your secret?" She said, "No. She wouldn't tell anyone my secrets!" I continued to push and push the other girl theory. She continued to say no she wouldn't say anything about me. I said she may have been using an example without your name and someone figured out that it was you she was talking about. No matter what I said, I could not shake her from her trust in her friend. She had an unshakable trust in her friend. She talked about the experiences they had gone through that developed that trust. She said that she had done things in the past that gave her reasons to share things about her friend but she kept them secret. She also said that she knew worse things about her to share, but I could not shake her from her trust in that friend.

Years later God reminded me about that conflict; how I couldn't shake her from her trust in her friend. God then asked me why I couldn't trust Him that same way, to have an unshakable trust in Him? God reminded me of the experiences He has brought me through in which I learned to wait (trust in the Lord). The more experiences we have, the more we learn to patiently wait and, thereby, trust God. The scripture says that tribulations work patience. When we are going through a problem (tribulation) it is easier to try and make things happen with our own strength. Manipulating, like Abraham, we too can create an Ishmael because we don't wait on God. This means that we are trying to bring a physical solution to a spiritual problem.

MANIPULATION

When we don't trust God we try to manipulate people to try to make things happen for us. We say God is in control but we try to manipulate or influence those around us. The Message Bible (MSG) says in Matthew 5:37, "When you manipulate words to get your own way, you go wrong." Also in Romans 14:23, "... for whatsoever is not of faith is sin." We pray God's will be done! But we manipulate those around us to get our will to be done. The world is in the state that it is in because people want their own way! The root of sin is selfishness. I have found that the more people trust God the less they manipulate others. But I have found the opposite to be true as well. The less people trust God the more they manipulate those around them. They lean on their own understanding. Controlling people are manipulative people. Proverb 3:5, "Trust in the Lord with all thine heart and lean not unto thine own understanding." I have seen people work harder to manipulate people to get something that would have taken less work and less pay. Psalm 20:7 (AMP), "Some trust in chariots and some in horses, but we will remember and trust in the name of the Lord our God. In other words, some trust in power some trust in money, but I will remember and trust in the Lord.

Manipulation can be as bold as prostitution, or as discreet as a smile. The only difference between manipulating someone and motivating someone is the intent. One's intention is a matter of the heart. People talk about others pushing their buttons. I tell my kids in the high school I work in to get rid of the button. I tell them that people don't go fishing where the fish aren't biting. They only go fishing where they can catch fish. When you stop biting on the bait they will stop fishing in your area. We look at their actions, but we need to look at ourselves and determine what is the cause of that button being there. Matthews 7:1 says, "Judge not, that ye be not judged." I change the word judge to correct. Correct yourself and no one will have to correct you! No one can push your button.

We can also determine if we trust God by our acts of manipulation. We have to look at our actions and ask, "Am I doing this to better them or for God!" Or am I doing this to get something for myself? In I Samuel 15:23, the Word of God says, "For rebellion is as the sin of witchcraft, and stubbornness is as iniquity and idolatry. Because thou hast rejected the word of the Lord, he hath also rejected thee from being king." Saul went by what he saw (walked by sight not faith in God). He trusted in what he saw not what God said. He didn't want to wait on God. Once we learn patience, because waiting is learning to trust God, we also gain experience.

EXPERIENCE

There is a saying, "The best teacher is experience." I remember in high school, as a gymnast, we learned how to flip. It was kind of a strange feeling going backward, but once I learned how I could do flips, you couldn't stop me; I did flip-flops everywhere. My mother coined the term "Gymnaskit-it!" because I did gymnastics everywhere--experience. As a young kid, we spent our summers at the neighborhood swimming pool. Once we showed the lifeguard that we could swim across the width of the pool we were allowed in the deep end of the pool. The pool had two diving boards, a high dive, and a low dive. My friends and I began jumping off the low diving board. We learned to dive and some learned to flip off the low diving board. But a few of my friends began to jump from the high diving board. Even some of my more timid friends began to jump from the high dive. I climbed up several times without jumping off. The rule was you could only climb up the ladder, not down it, but after my stay on the board for so long the lifeguard would say, "Byrd come down." My friends made fun of me and talked about me badly for not jumping. They would say, "Byrd! How can you be a bird and be afraid of heights?" I would climb up, walk to the end of the board and look down and say to myself, "No way! I can't do it!" But eventually, my friends stopped making fun of me; they started to encourage me saying, "You can do it!" Once I did jump off the high diving board, I began to cut people in line to jump off the high dive! The best teacher is experience because experience develops confidence. Once I did jump, it gave me the confidence to keep jumping. Experience! Because of our experiences, we gain confidence. When we don't get experience, a lot of times in life we don't go for things because of a lack of confidence. Some people don't apply for jobs because they believe they are not qualified. Some don't go to college because they don't think they can finish. But the fact is, they don't have confidence and experience; confidence is what we need to go forward. Experiences that we have in trusting in God develops confidence in God or trust in God. I believe God wants us all to have an unshakable trust in Him.

    Job had an unshakable trust in God! Job is one of the few people in the Bible that God bragged on. Job 2:3 (KJV) reads, "And the LORD said unto Satan, Hast thou considered my servant Job, that there is none like him in the earth, a perfect and an upright man, one that feareth God, and escheweth evil…" We can conclude that Job had faith seeing that God bragged on him! Hebrews 11:6 (KJV) reads, "But without faith it is impossible to please him: for he that cometh to God must believe that he is, and that he is a rewarder of them that diligently seek him." I believe that Job learned to trust God. Job 1:3 says about Job that he had a very great household; so that this man was the greatest of all the men of the east." I believe Job had faith and grew to trust God for his sons and daughters. I believe Job had faith and grew to trust God for his seven thousand sheep! I believe Job had faith and grew to trust God for his three thousand camels! I believe Job had faith and grew to trust God for his five hundred yokes of oxen, and five hundred she asses! Job had so many experiences of trusting God that his trust was unshakable. Job 2:9-10 (KJV) reads, "Then said his wife unto him, Dost thou still retain thine integrity? curse God, and die. But he said unto her, Thou speakest as one of the foolish women speaketh. What? shall we receive good at the hand of God, and shall we not receive evil? In all this did not Job sin with his lips." I change the word receive to trust in the tenth verse; "shall we *trust* (only) good at the hand of God, and shall we not trust God in evil?" I believe Job's trust in God grew to the point where Job said, "Though he slay me, yet will I trust in him... (Job 13:15)." I have come to appreciate all the accomplishments I have achieved so far with the help of God as I look to achieve more expectantly (hope). I feel grateful about what I already have experienced which makes me feel hopeful. I don't believe God brought me this far to leave me which gives me a positive expectation for the future (hope).

HOPEFULNESS

Experience (or confidence) gives us hope. What is hope? Hope is a positive expectation; belief that some good is coming to pass. Once we get experience (achievements) on something, we have a positive expectation about achieving it in the future. We can choose to let our limitations destroy our expectations! The enemy (the devil) is trying to destroy your potential. Satan tries to magnify our limitations to decrease our expectations. "Now faith is the substance of things hoped for, the evidence of things not seen. If hope is positive expectations then faith is the substance of things expected; it is the evidence of things not seen. Sports have taught me that the harder I work to win, the better my chances of winning. In that, expectation without work is just wishful thinking. There is a difference between a wish and a goal; with goals (expectations) you have to have a strategy or plan of how you are going to get it. Wishing just wants it to happen somehow. I believe that God wants to have our expectations destroy our limitations, and/ our expectations destroy our insecurities!

We show our insecurities by answering when someone calls us out of our names. One girl calls the other girl that negative word and wants to fight her to prove to her that she is not that negative word. But by trying to prove that she is not, she is really showing that she is. A person calls another person crazy. The other person gets mad and tries to prove that he/she is not crazy. But by trying to prove that he/she is not, they are really showing that he/she is. God wants to give you a royal identity. I will talk later about a new identity.

Matthews 15:11 says, "Not that which goeth into the mouth defileth (poisons) a man; but that which cometh out of the mouth, this defileth (poisons) a man." Young people listen to music that calls women the "B" word or the "WH" word. When they repeat the words, they poison themselves. According to Psalm 109:17 (KJV), "As he loved cursing, so let it come unto him: as he delighted not in blessing, so let it be far from him." That same verse in the Amplified Bible, says "He also loved cursing, and it came [back] to him; He did not delight in blessing, so it was far from him."

Matthews 15:11 says, "Not that which goeth into the mouth defileth (poisons) a man; but that which cometh out of the mouth, this defileth (poisons) a man." But in **Proverbs 15:4 (AMP)** A gentle tongue [with its healing power] is a tree of life, but willful contrariness in it breaks down the spirit. Our words can either heal or destroy! Death and life are in the power of our word! Our words are expressions of what is in our heart according to Matthew 12:34 and Luke 6:45.

Proverbs 4:23 (NIV) says, "Above all else, guard your heart, for everything you do flows from it." We have to guard what we let into our spirit; for what we allow in our spirit affects our spirit. When I first began doing crisis intervention counseling in inner-city schools, close to 30 years ago; if I did three suicide risk assessments a year, it was a busy year. In the last three years, there has been a day where I had three in one day. I have also had four risk assessments in one day. I believe that some of the contributing factors that are allowed to impact us include violent music, TV, and video games. I believe the only power the devil has over our lives is the power we give him! Genesis 3:1 (AMP) explains, that the serpent was more crafty (subtle, skilled in deceit) . . . and like the forbidden fruit, we take it in thinking it is okay for us!

God had been dealing with me so much about hope. The Message Bible reads in I Corinthians 13:13, "But for right now, until that completeness, we have three things to do to lead us toward that consummation: Trust steadily in God, hope unswervingly, love extravagantly. And the best of the three is love." I knew the importance of faith, for without it we can't please God. According to Hebrews 11:6, I see the importance of love, our only commandment. But sandwiched between these two necessary things is hope! I have so much to say about hope; it could be a book all by itself. But I want to keep the focus on the attitude of gratitude, true worship. Working in an inner-city school, I have found that many kids have no hope! "Learned hopelessness!" They have no positive expectations for the future. There is an expression, "Laugh now cry later!" when people see no future they try to make the best of "right now" regardless of the pain it will cause in the future. Kids that do drugs know personally the danger of drugs more than anyone, but yet they still do drugs because of a lack of hope (no positive expectations)! Kids that join gangs know personally the danger of being in a gang more than anyone but they stay in gangs because they lack hope (no positive expectations)! I have noticed over the years that God has given me messages of hope to help people overcome more than anything else. With a positive expectation in God, we can do things; God can do anything. We must have an attitude of faith, for Hebrews 11:6 says, "But without faith it is impossible to please Him: …". Worship is our expression of trusting God as well as our love of God. But without faith we can't please God. Faith or trusting God is vital to having an attitude of thankfulness. We can say as David did in Psalm 27:13 (KJV), "I had fainted, unless I had believed (hope) to see the goodness of the LORD in the land of the living (or as I live)." If our expectation is greater than our tribulations; we will overcome any tribulation. The greater our tribulation gets, the greater we should raise our expectations in God. In short, we must have positive expectation in God to truly worship. Romans 8:37 (NKJV), "Yet in all these things we are more than conquerors through Him who loved us." Therefore, we must overcome doubts for James 1:7 teaches, "For let not that man (that doubts) think that he shall receive anything of the Lord."

OVERCOMING DOUBTS

The Bible says in James 1:6-8 (NIV), "But when you ask, you must believe and not doubt, because the one who doubts is like a wave of the sea, blown and tossed by the wind. 7) <u>That person should not expect to receive anything from the Lord</u>. 8) Such a person is double-minded and unstable in all they do." We can ask and have no expectation and not receive from God. God wants us to get to the point where we have a positive expectation and a hope. When we totally trust in God, we know and experience that God has done it before and that God can do it again. We learned to have patience. We learned to trust. This gives us experience that leads us to positive expectations because He did it before and He will do it again.

To truly worship God we must overcome our doubts. I believe the enemy (the devil) is working overtime to create doubts in our minds to destroy our faith, thereby demolishing our worship. Revelation 12:11 reads, "And they overcame him by the blood of the Lamb, and by the word of their testimony; and they loved not their lives unto the death." In other words, they overcame by what

Jesus did on the cross, by what they said (testimony) and by their willingness to die for Christ. We overcome doubts by what we say to ourselves.

Students with depression and/or anxiety come to my office feeling like they can't stop thinking negative thoughts. I ask them to imagine an elephant and tell them that whatever they do, don't let the image of the elephant disappear. I ask them to focus on its trunk, the gray color and the roughness of the skin. I then ask them to say their names out loud. Next, I ask what happened to the elephant when they said their names; they responded that it disappeared. I then tell them that what they say out loud has more power than what they think. Death and life are in the power of the tongue! We overcome our negative thoughts by the blood of Jesus and the words of our testimony (what we say). We should say God did it before; God will do it again. God did it for them, He will do it for me. 1 Corinthians 10:11 expresses, "Now all these things happened unto them, for example: and they are written for our admonition, upon whom the ends of the world are come." I used to say our mouth is the gun and the words spoken from God's word are the (admonition) bullets. Now I say our mouths are the missile launchers and our words are the missiles. We are not just killing our enemy, we are destroying all the works of the enemy. We can have the best weapon but no admonition, which leaves us defenseless; we should say, "didn't you once dry up the sea, the powerful waters of the deep, and then make the bottom of the ocean a road for the redeemed to walk across?" Isaiah 51:10 (MSG) declares, "I believe worship is our admonition wherewith we defeat the enemy." II Corinthians 4:15 (AMP) asserts, "For all [these] things are [taking place] for your sake, so that the more grace (divine favor and spiritual blessing) extends to more and more people and multiplies through the many, that more thanksgiving may increase [and redound] to the glory of God.

Earlier I talked about Job and how he grew to trust God. I believe the same can be said about Abraham. Romans 4:19-20 (KJV) declares, "And being not weak in faith, he considered not his own body now dead, when he was about a hundred years old, neither yet the deadness of Sara's womb: 20 He staggered not at the promise of God through unbelief; but was strong in faith, <u>giving glory to God</u>." The more we worship "<u>giving glory to God</u>" the more our trust grows. Abraham was also rich and God also bragged on him. The Bible speaks of his faith in God. I believe his faith grew as his trust in God grew because he trusted God for more and more. I use these examples as my admonition; God did it before; God will do it again! God will do the same for me!

In Colossians 3:15, it reads, "And let the peace of God rule in your hearts, to the which also ye are called in one body; and be ye thankful." We can let God's peace rule (control) our hearts or not. I have found the more I trust God the more peace I have! The less I trust God the less peace I have! For as many members we are all in one body, we are all called to live in peace. That is a total contradiction of the world standards; the Bible says God is not the author of confusion. We live in a dualistic world. There is a kingdom of darkness and there is a kingdom of light. Which one are we participating in when we allow confusion, frustration, anger, and bitterness to take control of our hearts?

We must allow the peace of God to rule our hearts. We are all called to live in peace and the last thing it says is always be thankful (have an attitude of gratitude), but how do we do this, how can we show that we are thankful? In Ephesians 5:19 it reads, "**Speaking to yourselves** in songs and hymns and spiritual songs." We should be praising God, worshipping God, and always giving thanks for all things. We can be thankful in tribulations; it's what we focus on. When we think about the negatives we attract the negatives, which is what hinders us from being thankful? It is important to document (write down) what we are thankful for. But I also see the importance of "speaking to yourself." The person you listen to more than anyone is yourself! The person you trust more than anyone is yourself! When you speak negative you trust your words! But you trust your words when you speak positively as well! "Faith comes by hearing and hearing by the Word of God", exhorts Romans 10:17.

THERE ARE TWO KINDS OF PEOPLE

I was told and I believe, "There are two kinds of people"; people that think there is only so much, and because others have more, there is less for them. Then there are people that think God is a God of abundance. There is always enough! I believe God has enough to bless everyone and still have leftovers. I believe that God can give us more than we can contain, the overflow, which causes us to be blessed and we can give the rest to others. God will give us more than we will ever use in a lifetime. He will bless us so much that we have to bless others around us because it's just too much for us.

One thing that I have seen that hinders people's blessings is their mindsets--it's in our thinking. We can be set free but still keep a slave-like mindset. David went through trials and tribulations, but he was thankful. Job went through, as well, and he was also thankful. I once asked God why people are so blessed and I began to visualize a father on one side of a big front yard watering the grass. Boys were running around playing tag. The older boys asked the father to put water on them? The father said, "go and play;

can't you see that I'm working?" But as one of the younger boys was running around and got wet slightly, the other younger boys got excited saying, "Joey is getting wet! Joey got wet!" The more excited the younger boys got the more water the father sprayed on them. They were saying, "Joey and Sam got wet! Joey, Sam and David got wet!" The more the younger boys got excited, the more water was sprayed out on them! The more the younger got happy the more the older boys got mad. They said, "Why didn't we get wet, we are the ones who asked to get wet! That's not fair! We are the ones who should get wet!" The more excited the younger boys got about someone else being blessed (wet) the more they got blessed (wet). As I was thinking about how the older kids took themselves out of the flow of God's blessing, God said to me, "The kids are more important than the grass!" He wants to bless everyone but it's our attitude that takes us out of the flow of God's blessing. The blessing is in our thankfulness to God. The older kids left ungrateful and took themselves out of the flow of God's blessings. We, too, take ourselves out of the flow of God's blessing by complaining; why did they get something and I didn't! I am now happy for others when they get blessed and I see that the window of heaven has opened to them. I praise God for them so that the window may remain open for me. This revelation (and change of perception) changed my life and I hope it will change your perception as well.

SOWING AND REAPING

Galatians 6:7 reads, "Be not deceived; God is not mocked: for <u>whatsoever</u> a man soweth, that shall he also reap. God is not mocked! We can't fool God! Another way of saying sowing is broadcasting. Another word for reaping is producing. Whatever you broadcast you produce. If you broadcast wants and needs, you produce more wants and needs. If you produce thanksgiving and gratitude you produce more to be thankful for; the blessings from God. God is trying to tell us whatever you think and talk about you bring about, whatever we sow (broadcasting), we produce. I used to say I don't have money. I didn't know I was sowing lack and need. But I knew I was reaping lack and needs in my life! I was set free but I kept a slave mentality. That was why I continued to produce lack. Sowing and reaping apply to more than money. I have found that more has to do with our attitude and the experiences we have gone through.

The more you put into anything the more you get out of it. Psalm 109:17 (GW) says, "He loved to put curses {on others}, so he, too, was cursed. He did not like to bless {others}, so he never received a blessing." We can't give anything to God that He has not already given us, but we can give to God's people. When we bless God's people we bless God. This is what I call the law of blessing and cursing. James 3:9-10 (GW), "With our tongues, we praise our Lord and Father. Yet, with the same tongues, we curse people, who were created in God's likeness. 10) Praise and curses come from the same mouth. My brothers and sisters, <u>this should not happen</u>!" I believe when praises go up God's blessings come down. But because we curse others we receive curses, not blessings. The world understands and practices *The Law of Reciprocity*. "When you give out you receive more in return." But many believers don't receive blessings coming down to them, because of their blaming, complaining and putting others down. We live in a negative world with a lot of people with negative attitudes. Being positive and worshiping God is like swimming upstream (going against the flow). Changing our attitude to that of being thankful takes a lot of effort. This is why I encourage the daily writing and saying out loud things for which you are thankful. You create new positive neuropathways. Your new positive thoughts become stronger than your old negative ones. When we sow cursing of others we reap curses on ourselves. But a more powerful truth is when you bless others God blesses you! I believe we should tell people that we are thankful for the things they do. We should bless them by showing them we are thankful for them being in our lives.

Hurting people hurt people! When people have difficulty moving beyond their past pain they have difficulty truly worshiping and giving God the praise.

THERE IS A PURPOSE BEHIND OUR PAIN

I'd like to change your perception about the problems in life. I believe the hurtful issues in life can either help us or hold us back. The biggest determiner of our success is not the hurtful issues in life but how we deal with the hurtful issues. Is this pain here to help me or hurt me? I look back on my life and I can truly say I thank God for the punishment I received as a child. The punishment I received is now considered child abuse. There was a saying I heard growing up, "I am beating you so the police won't get to!" In that, the pain I experienced would strongly influence my choices before I did something stupid. I have seen where painful issues both helped people and situations where it hurt them.

In counseling and working with people, I have found the biggest problem that stops people from moving beyond the painful issues and to have an attitude of gratitude and truly worship is the question, "Why did this happen to me?" They feel they can't truly be thankful because they think God is mad at them. They question God! I believe God allows pain to increase your greatness based on Psalms 71:21. I have come to understand that there really is a divine design to every experience. No matter how painful, every experience is a reflection of something we need to know about ourselves. There is a purpose behind our pain. Hebrews 12:2 says, "Jesus . . . for the joy that was set before him endured the cross." Also, Romans 8:28 says, "And we know that God causes everything to work together for the good of those who love God."

As I conducted drug and alcohol counseling in the past, I questioned why some people have greater struggles than others and why some were instantly healed through deliverance from drugs but others were healed through disciplining themselves. Some people were healed and walked after an injury through a miraculous deliverance while others struggled and learned to walk again after an injury from disciplining themselves.

The answer I believe I have found is that God wants to develop more character in some people that they will need later for leadership. A preacher once told me a vivid story of how he developed character during his difficulties while going through basic training, and later of his survival in the jungle during guerrilla warfare. While he was going through basic training, he felt like they pushed him, as well as others, too hard. He felt like they were stressing and exhausting him for no reason, but the things that he hated doing were the things that kept him alive in the jungle. I see that the struggles that he endured during his basic training prepared him for his survival and later success in life. God caused those things to work for his good! He told a story of a shelling (bombing) in the jungle where he ran to the place where the bomb had just exploded. He believed that if a bomb had exploded in an area that it would be a long time before another bomb would hit in that area again. He saw people run into an explosion trying to escape from an explosion. Often we run into an explosion trying to run from an explosion. I have seen people running into hurt trying to run from hurt.

Young people use a term to describe people going from one stupid situation to the next stupid situation. They call it, "stuck on stupid." Their hurts of the past are motivating their stupid behaviors. We, not like the pastor, don't like to face the destruction and find safety where the bomb has recently exploded. Likewise, we don't like to face the hurt others have caused in our lives. I have seen people running from hurts and run into hurts. I believe they would stop running into hurts if they would only stop and face the hurts. Forgiveness! Romans 5:3-5 (NKJV) reads, "Knowing that tribulation [suffering] produces perseverance, and perseverance, character, and character, hope. Now hope [positive expectations] does not disappoint."

We, too, can endure the painful experiences to enjoy the strength in character we gain through those experiences. I define character as "inner strength." I believe this is one of the purposes behind our pain. A way for Christians to reframe our hurts is to realize that there is a purpose behind our pain. I believe David reframed his pain. Psalm 71:20-21 (KJV) reads, "Thou which has shown me great and sore troubles shalt quicken me again and shalt bring me up again from the depth of the earth. Thou shalt increase my greatness, and comfort me on every side." I believe God wants to increase your greatness TO WHICH I HAVE MANY EXAMPLES! I have counseled a young man who was angry with God because of the pain he had endured. The pain developed the character or charisma he needed to lead other young men out of a life of gangs and violence. I have counseled a young lady who was raised by her grandmother. She, too, was angry with God at the death of her grandmother. Because of her pain, she began working with ladies who were making bad choices in their lives, but because of her character and charisma, she was able to help those young ladies make better choices.

That is the kind of character that God wants! Just like friends learn to trust one another, we have to learn to trust God. Therefore, God gives us experiences with struggles and pains where we learn to trust Him. Our trust in God grows when we obey Him by forgiving those who hurt us.

Another purpose behind our pain is to help others. Second Corinthians 1:4 says, "Who comforteth us in all our tribulation, <u>that we may be able to comfort them which are in any trouble</u>, by the comfort wherewith we ourselves are comforted of God."

We are God's representatives here on earth; we are to show or represent God's love and forgiveness to others. We have to forgive others to have and keep an attitude of gratitude to have true worship. Jesus taught us to pray, "Thy kingdom come, thy will be done". God's will is for us to have love and forgiveness for one another. It is also God's will for us to be thankful. I believe hurts and unforgiveness hinders true worship. Unforgiveness hinders our intimacy with God. Matthew 5:23-25 states, "Therefore if thou bring thy gift to the altar, and there rememberest that thy brother hath ought against thee; 24) Leave there thy gift before the altar and go thy way; first be reconciled to thy brother, and then come and offer thy gift." Also, in Mark 11:24-25 (KJV) it reads, "Therefore I say unto you, What things soever ye desire, when ye pray, believe that ye receive them, and ye shall have them. 25) And when ye stand praying, forgive, if ye have ought against any: that your Father also which is in heaven may forgive you your trespasses." The conjunction "and" makes forgiveness mandatory for answered prayers.

The scriptures say in everything give thanks: for this is the will of God in Christ Jesus concerning you. Not only in good times should we be thankful but also in the bad times as well.

I don't know if you have ever experienced the anger and frustration of missing a connecting flight. My wife and I were on vacation and were taking a cruise out of Puerto Rico. Our flight required a transfer in Fort Lauderdale, Florida. We walked nearly all the way across the airport to the gate only to find that we had to go back across the airport to another gate. Once we reached that gate, the airplane doors were closed. We missed our flight.

Michael Byrd Ph.D.

There were no other flights from that airline to that city that day. We were told about other airlines that had flights out that day so we walked back across the airport and talked to another airline about a ticket so that we could board the ship before it set sail. The first price was $240.00 for both of us. But then the person realized that the flight left from another airport. The ticket price for both of us from their airline was $428.00 but if we didn't take that flight, we would miss the ship and lose thousands of dollars from missing the cruise. So we paid for the tickets and waited. The flight was delayed six times. Each time it was delayed, my flesh wanted to get angry and blame it on the airline. Upon hearing of the fifth delay, we said that if the plane would land on time that we could make it. After the sixth delay, all hope was lost; but, I kept singing, Tye Tribbett's "Better". All we had were a change of clothes and toiletries in our carry-on bags. Our clothes were on the original departing flight to Puerto Rico. We flew in but our bags could not be picked up until the airline opened at noon. The airline gave us a free hotel night for the delay and for missing our ship. We stayed the night in Puerto Rico and every time I had negative thoughts come to try to steal my peace I would sing to myself Tribbett's "Better." The next morning we woke up early to go from airline to airline looking for a flight to St. Thomas, the cruises next destination. All the airlines were full or only had one seat available. It all looked hopeless. I kept singing to myself, "Being with you Makes All Things Better; Living with you Makes all Things Better. My wife was persistent and found an airline going to St. Thomas. It would land in time for us to take a cab to the ship. Well, we made it to the ship and enjoyed the rest of the cruise. I don't think we would have made it if I hadn't continued to worship God! He made it better! It took a lot of trust in God! But my trust in God grew. All during this ordeal, I had to continue to pray for the airline and forgive them so my flesh wouldn't lash out. I had a choice to either go by what it looked like or walk in faith! Allow the peace of God to rule my heart or allow anger to create an atmosphere of anger. I saw others cursing the airlines.

We can create an atmosphere of love and hope (positive expectations) or allow the enemy to create an atmosphere of hurts and counter-hurts where hurting people hurt others, which eventually creates an atmosphere of crime and violence. In certain parts of America, it has become a war zone! Hurting people hurt people! Hurting people also complain! People allow their pain to become larger than their God. This is why I believe that our character is so important to God. Romans 8:28 says, "**And we know** that God causes everything to work together for the good of those who love God and are called according to his purpose for them." When we don't know if things will work out we get angry and blame and complain.

If we look at the heroes of the Bible, we see godly men and women going through struggles and coming out stronger. Joseph the dreamer, even in his struggles of life, and how he forgave his brothers for selling him into slavery, came out stronger. David also showed forgiveness when he had an opportunity to get revenge on Saul but, "David said to Abishai, Destroy him not: for who can stretch forth his hand against the Lord's anointed" (1 Sam. 26:9). In my lifetime, I have had examples of walking in forgiveness and becoming stronger.

The biggest is Dr. Martin Luther King Jr., who, I believe, was one of the most charismatic people of the twentieth century. I believe his charisma was developed by going through the struggles. God causes those things to work for our good! People are not born with charisma; it is developed through life's difficulties. People are drawn to people with charisma. Dr. King's charisma helped him to lead people to lay their lives on the line by demonstrating during the fight for civil rights. Who knows—the pain that you are going through or have gone through may give you the drawing power that leads someone to Christ.

Many of the most charismatic people on radio, television, and movies today have a story of pains and hurts before becoming famous. I believe it was those hurts and pains that created the charisma in their lives. People living on the streets or in prison have similar stories, but their outcomes are polar opposites. You can allow your hurts to <u>make you or break you with God's help</u>! This is the reason we need to forgive. Another reason for the pain is to show us our true selves. If I'm walking bear-footed and stomp my toes and curse words come out my mouth; the stomping of my toe didn't put the curse words in my mouth. It just revealed what was in my heart. Pain sometimes comes to show us ourselves. Pain reveals what is truly in our hearts. Pressure from the outside squeezes us to bring out what is in us. I have found that pain reveals what is in our hearts. If I have any pain and curse words come out of my mouth, the pain did not put the curse words in. It only showed me what was in my heart from the start. Pain reveals one's true character.

The question people without character often ask is, "Is it safe to trust God and walk in forgiveness in today's world?" With all the violence and crime today—child molestations, domestic violence, drive-by shootings, gangs and hate groups—violence is all we hear about. Not to mention the war on terrorism: should we forgive them and let these persons go unpunished?

Being ready and willing to forgive does not mean that we allow people to be unaccountable for their actions. Forgiveness suggests that people seek fairness by holding offenders accountable for their actions. I can forgive someone for shooting me with a gun, but just because I forgave him doesn't mean I should give him a gun so he can shoot me again or worse, shoot someone else. Just because you forgive someone doesn't mean that you have changed your name to Matt—short for doormat—in that people can walk all over you! You will have to forgive the person who sold you a lemon of a car, but you don't have to trust him or her and continue buying cars from him or her.

Once I counseled a wife of an abusive husband. The wife read my book and said, "I have to forgive him when he apologizes." She explained that her husband told her that he only hit her because she made him mad and that he wouldn't hit her if she didn't make him mad! I told her that he did not apologize for hitting her; he justified why he hit her. I also told her that any sin we can justify we will repeat because we made it okay to continue doing it by justifying it. We must pray for others but not be preyed upon by others. Can you imagine the world without consequences? Imagine a world where people can do anything regardless of the hurt or harm it causes to others.

During the question-and-answer time when I speak at conferences, I am often asked about divorce from a physically abusive mate. Can a person divorce because of abuse? I have seen God lead people to stay in an abusive marriage, which led the mate to Christ. I also have seen God release people through divorce. I believe we should be dogmatic about what the Bible is dogmatic about and not dogmatic about the things the Bible is not dogmatic about. The Bible only makes allowances for unfaithfulness. Matthew 19:6 says, "What therefore God hath joined together, let not man put asunder." But the Bible also talks about how we are to be good stewards of everything God has given us, including our bodies and their safety.

If the scripture does not give clear directions, we must seek God's direction in the matter. We have to be led by the Spirit. I encourage people to give the situation the test of love. All our actions should be motivated by love. Am I divorcing him/her because of hurt and anger or because I need to protect what God has invested in me? The question people ask going through divorce is what is God's will? Give thanks! I also encourage them to seek counsel from their pastor, their spiritual covering. His or her job is to lead you in the right direction. I encourage people to spend time with God, listening for His direction.

I'd like to, again, emphasize the fact that it takes courage and strength to forgive. Someone may knock you down, but unforgiveness keeps you down. Forgiveness, on the other hand, stands you back up. When you acknowledge that you have been victimized, you break the chains of psychological slavery.

I have also seen where receiving forgiveness helps people become free from psychological slavery. I always tell people, "Hurting people hurt people!" I know of a married couple where, because the wife was abused by her father as a child, she subconsciously did things to hurt her husband. Her unforgiveness of her father was sabotaging her relationship with her husband. Although she regretted hurting her husband, she continued to find herself hurting him over and over again. She was using her husband to unconsciously get back at her father. The husband, because he knew of the childhood abuse, responded by representing her heavenly Father with unconditional love. Through his act of unconditional love, she learned to forgive her father, which resulted in healing in her life.

When one continues to walk in forgiveness, it frees one from the emotional bondage that holds others back. Be ready and willing to forgive as different issues and situations come up so you will continue in the freedom that forgiveness gave you. No longer allow yourself to become entangled in the bondage of unforgiveness. Hurting people hurt people! Blessed people bless people! Blessed people also bless God and praise and worship Him.

One night I was halfway asleep. I dreamed or visualized two teams were competing on a football field. One team was the Angels of God and the other was the Fallen Angels. I was part of the audience. The more I and the crowd worshiped and praised God, the more the Angels of God advanced. But the more we just sat and watched, the more the Fallen Angels advanced. The more we complained, the more the Fallen Angels advanced and scored.

We want to win spiritual battles but we like to complain, thereby giving Satan the victory.

We must bless God and bless God's people! We do spiritual warfare when we worship, but we also conduct warfare when we complain. I believe David did spiritual warfare all through the Psalms. In Psalm 8:2 (NIV), "Through the praise of children and infants you have established <u>a stronghold against your enemies</u>, to silence the foe and the avenger. Psalm 9:1 (NIV), proclaims, "I will give thanks to you, LORD, with all my heart; I will tell of all your wonderful deeds." To war in the spirit we have to know the authority we have in our new identity in Christ.

NEW IDENTITY IN CHRIST

We are reborn. We are born again to worship God. One's identity (how a person sees themselves, think about themselves, and how they feel about themselves) determines their destination. According to Proverbs 23:7 (KJV), "For as he thinketh in his heart, so is he." In psychology, the term is called self-fulfilling prophecy! As a person believes, so he/she becomes. We are set free or enslaved by what we say, think and do. Again, most people's conflict with others stems from their insecurities. One white person calls a black person that N-word and wants to fight them to prove that they are not the N-word. But by trying to prove that they are not, they really are showing that they are. A person calls another person stupid. The other person gets mad and tries to prove that they are not stupid. But by trying to prove that they are not, they really are showing that they are. God wants to give you a royal identity.

II Corinthians 5:17, "Therefore if any man be in Christ, he is a new creature: old things are passed away; behold, all things are become new. Acts 11:26 (KJV), "The disciples were called Christians first in Antioch." They were called Christian or Christ-like because they acted like Christ. They said the things Jesus said, and they did the things Jesus did! They identified themselves with Christ. They received a new identity in Christ. Ephesians 2:10 (AMP) states, "For we are God's [own] handiwork (His workmanship), recreated in Christ Jesus, [born anew] that we may do those good works which God predestined (planned beforehand) for us [taking paths which He prepared ahead of time], that we should walk in them [living the good life which He prearranged and made ready for us to live]. We can be set free but keep a slave mentality! We can be recreated in Christ Jesus, born anew, but be drawn back to an old way of thinking! God wants us to walk in good works which He predestined us to walk in. We have a choice! But God knows the choice we will make. God pre-knew the ones that would say yes to His will. I remember at age 16 I gave my life to God. I remember cleaning up the kitchen for what seemed like months. I heard my father say to my next to the oldest brother to clean the kitchen. An argument with cursing followed and my brother slammed the door as he left. I then heard my father ask my younger brother to clean the kitchen, an argument with cursing followed and my youngest brother slammed the door as he left. My father then came to me and asked me to clean the kitchen, I imagined myself much older in the kitchen cleaning up after my brothers. I said, "No dad, I've been cleaning up after everyone for weeks, it's not fair!" As I was sitting in my room, God began to speak to me. God said, "You need to apologize to your father and clean the kitchen." I began to argue with God. But God kept saying, "You need to apologize to your father and clean the kitchen." I then cleaned the kitchen and apologized to my father. Years later in my adult life God reminded me of that situation. God said the only reason why my father asked me to clean the kitchen was that my father knew I would do it. He knew I would say yes to Him! God knows who will say yes to His will, who will conform to the image of His Son! Deuteronomy

30:19 (KJV) says, "I call heaven and earth to record this day against you, that I have set before you life and death, blessing and cursing: therefore choose life, that both thou and thy seed may live. We always have a choice! Because our identity (how we see ourselves) determines our destiny in life. We don't know our future but God knows. God knows whether or not you will. "Be not conformed to this world", for the Word says, "but be ye transformed by the renewing of your mind, that ye may prove what is that good, and acceptable, and perfect, will of God", Romans 12:2. God wants to transform our thinking to kingdom thinking!

We have to grow into our new identity in Christ. I recall making mistakes in my identity. I was a young Christian in high school with other white Christians and the topic came up about us being Jewish because we have been circumcised in the heart. They said all Christians are Jews. I kept saying, "No I'm black." I was set free but I wanted to keep my old identity. About 25 years later working in ministry driving down the street I saw a black man driving a Cadillac with a sign saying, "SOLD OUT". I got mad saying to myself why would someone say that they are a sell out to anyone? God began to deal with me about giving Him everything; being totally SOLD OUT!

We see the importance of having a God Kingdom identity in Matthew 22:2-14 (KJV), "The kingdom of heaven is like unto a certain king, which made a marriage for his son, 3) And sent forth his servants to call them that were bidden to the wedding: and they would not come. 4) Again, he sent forth other servants, saying, Tell them which are bidden, Behold, I have prepared my dinner: my oxen and my fatlings are killed, and all things are ready: come unto the marriage. 5) But they made light of it, and went their ways, one to his farm, another to his merchandise: 6) And the remnant took his servants, and entreated them spitefully, and slew them. 7) But when the king heard thereof, he was wroth: and he sent forth his armies, and destroyed those murderers, and burned up their city. 8) Then saith he to his servants, the wedding is ready, but they which were bidden were not worthy. 9) Go ye therefore into the highways, and as many as ye shall find, bid to the marriage. 10) So those servants went out into the highways, and gathered together as many as they found, both bad and good: and the wedding was furnished with guests. 11) And when the king came in to see the guests, he saw there a man which had not on a wedding garment: 12) And he saith unto him, Friend, how camest thou in hither not having a wedding garment? And he was speechless. 13) Then said the king to the servants, Bind him hand and foot, and take him away, and cast him into outer darkness; there shall be weeping and gnashing of teeth. 14) For many are called, but few are chosen." The wedding garment identified you as a subject of the king. It was not just disrespectful to not wear the wedding garment but it was thought of as treachery (rebellion). To reject being identified with the king and his kingdom was thought of as treachery. We always have a choice to not take on the life of Christ, rejecting God's Identity. Our identity determines our destination, both naturally and spiritually. As we give thanks we conform to God's image.

OUR LIVES HAVE A TENDENCY TO GO TOWARD THE DIRECTION WE FOCUS

When Drivers' Ed. teachers teach new drivers on the road for the first time, the new driver will see a car coming toward them in the opposite lane and will begin to go toward the direction of the oncoming car because we have a tendency to go toward what we focus on. Our lives have a tendency to go toward the direction we focus on. I remember during college learning how to ride a motorcycle. Years later, a friend got a new motorcycle. It had been a few years since I'd driven one, but I thought, I'll go slow. I was turning a corner slowly and I looked to the side to where I didn't want to go. I then fell off the bike in the direction I was looking. The problem is I didn't learn from that. Years later I was on a dirt bike on a rocky trail going faster when turning a corner. When I began to look to where I didn't want to go, I fell again. This time it was painful enough for me to learn to always look to where I wanted to go. And never look to where I don't want to go. We have a tendency to go toward the direction we focus both naturally and spiritually. Our lives gravitate to what we focus on. 1 Timothy 4:16 (GW), "Focus on your life and your teaching. Continue to do what I've told you. If you do this, you will save yourself and those who hear you."

Life is like the game of baseball. If your batting average is 300 or better you are at the top of your game, in that most people are batting well below 300. But if you are batting 300 that means that 70% of the time you come to bat you get an out. The better batters focus on their successes, not their failures. They focus on their hits, not on their misses. The more they focus on their hits the better their chances of making a hit. The more they focus on their misses the greater their likelihood of missing. So, too, in all life's situations, the more we focus on the good things in life, the better the chances of good things happening. The more we focus on the bad things in life the better the chances of bad things happening. The children of Israel after seeing all the great miracles God did for them only focus on the small in comparison to problems they had to overcome. I believe Joshua and Caleb focused on the miracles God did for them.

I have students come into my office with $150 to $200 gym shoes and $100 shirts who want to talk to me about their depression. They only focus on what they don't have rather than what they have. Students with great things going on in their lives come to me about their anxiety. They focus on things they can't control rather than the things they are controlling. The problem is what they focus on. Brain chemistry does influence behavior but doesn't nullify one's choice. Medication can help with brain chemistry. But counseling is needed to reframe their thinking. Every thought and feeling is a chemical reaction in the brain. People that are chemically depressed have a problem with producing or receiving the chemical that makes one feel good; thereby trapping them into a cycle of negative thinking. There is no one that can live 15 or 16 years and have no good things happen in their lives; they wouldn't survive. It is what they focus on. Negative people focus on negative things in life. Positive people focus on the positive things in life! A person can have hundreds of great things going on in their lives but focus on one bad thing; leading to depression. Kids have said in counseling there is nothing good in my life. Arguing with them about it has a tendency to reinforce the negative belief system. Some counseling techniques are affirmations and gratitude lists. If you focus on lack you bring more lack, if you focus on thankfulness you bring more things to be thankful for. Focusing on the positive things in our lives helps. We have to be thankful. If someone gave us something of value the more valuable the thing, the more we will say good things about that person. The greater we value what they gave us the greater praise we will give them. The more we value God, the more we will praise God. The essence of praising God is being thankful, we praise God because of what he has done for us. We focus on all that God has blessed us with, not what we want or lack.

The core of praise and worship is being thankful to God for what he has done for us. It's what we focus on. Successful people focus on their successes. If you set goals, and achieve those goals, it provides more focus and determination to reach other goals. The opposite is true; the less you believe you can do it, the less you focus, the less your determination. It's all in the way a person believes. If you don't believe, you can then you won't try, which means that you are right. I have a sign on my office wall that says in bold letters, "Elevate your mind and you will go higher!" I believe God is trying to tell us it's what we focus on. Focusing on success leads to more success; if we focus on failure we reinforce failure. Some of the richest people have failed. But they focus on their successes. Also, the opposite is true! We have to focus on what God has given us not on what we don't have (reap and sow). Sometimes we have to fake it 'till we make it. We must say to ourselves yes we can when we believe we can't. There were times when I was going through things and I just kept saying that I trust you, Lord, when that was the furthest thing I was believing (but I would make myself believe). It didn't look like anything good was going to come out of it, and the reality is that I do think I changed the way I believed by what I said. We have to say God thank you. We can rejoice when we go through tribulations. There is a saying, "When praises go up, blessings come down!" they knew what they were talking about because they had experienced it. I have also found it true.

Gratitude can open up energy channels to receive abundance from God according to Psalm 9:1 (NIV). According to Psalm 9:1 (NIV), Praise is the essence of an attitude of gratitude, the more I think of the goodness of Jesus my heart cries out thank you, Jesus! When I think about His goodness and all that he has done for me I can't help but say hallelujah!--thank God for saving me. He took this little angry kid and He changed him. My friends got away with stealing while I got caught, but God changed this little angry kid. Now, I can't help but say Alleluia; which is the highest praise you can give to God.

When we think of what God has done for us it's what we focus on. I used to question why I would start praying for stuff, giving God praise, and going into worship. I feel it is because He deserves it! The Bible talks in the future tense, for example, we are healed, it's already done! If we're thankful, we have had some experience that gives us confidence that gives us a positive expectation. If we don't have the patience to wait on the Lord we will try to get out there and do it ourselves. I learned patience (waiting on God). I remember times in my life when I had no money. Things were so tight at times. Being a drug counselor, I knew some people who if I would have fronted them some money, I believed I would get a big return. I would not be directly selling but indirectly selling drugs by sponsoring a drug dealer. I told the Lord I would rather pick up and sell cans than sell poison. I've seen the devastation drugs have done to the families, communities, and to our country. I wanted to try to make it happen. Like Abraham with Ishmael, I was going to make the promises of God come true under my own strength. If we have patience, He will turn that into experience, then into confidence, then into hope and positive expectation. We will start to believe that no matter what happens God will bring us out! We praise God and blessings come down!

Did you know most babies will fall more times than they will take steps? But every time the baby does take a step and people around them cheer for them, the baby focuses on their successes; not their failures. If the baby focuses on the times it falls, it would become fearful and not try to walk. Confidence keeps us going forward; once we get experience, we get confidence. In Matthew 18:3 Jesus said, "Verily I say unto you, except ye be converted, and become as little children, ye shall not enter into the kingdom of heaven." We learn by taking baby steps in faith. Just as babies grow in confidence with each step they take we, too, should grow more confident in God. Confidence is one of the things we need in life, we have confidence in God.

I have been teaching, coaching, and counseling students for over 40 years. I have learned through experiences and observation that success in life is not rocket science. On the contrary, it is simply based on what people focus. I have seen a student that struggled in school but stayed focused (doing the things needed for their future success) on their future and later became successful. I have also seen a lot of the opposite in students that were smart and talented but focused on having fun now and ignoring the things that make their futures better. I have had students that say they want to graduate from high school but they are always skipping (or missing class.) I ask them how anyone can graduate from high school if they don't attend their classes. I have learned that success is simple. The more you focus on your future (do the things needed for their future) the better your future becomes. The opposite is true. The less you focus on your future (do the things needed for their future) the less you do that leads to future success. Think for a minute about the world's greatest archer. Do they just go up and shoot or do they focus on hitting the bullseye? Do you think that the harder they focus on hitting the bull's eye the better their chances of hitting it? So, too, is everything else in life, the harder you focus on hitting your targets or goals in life the better your chances of reaching them.

We have to focus to overcome distractions. Which is the better basketball player? The person that can make 80% of his free throws only when the gym is quiet with no distractions, or the person that can make 80% of his free throws with people yelling, screaming and waving long balloons behind the goal to distract him? Of course, it is the one that can stay focused in spite of the distractions. The question is which one of the two are you? An even better question is, which one do you want to be? The first step is to know where you are. If you think you are east from your target but really you are west of it, the more you go west the further you are going from your target. We have to take a realist look at our abilities to stay focused during distractions.

COMPLAINING VERSES WORSHIPING

I see a very close similarity between the children of Israel who didn't get into the Promised Land and Christians today. That similarity is the complaining. First Corinthians 10:9-10 reads, "Neither let us tempt Christ, as some of them also tempted, and were destroyed of serpents. Neither murmur ye, as some of them also murmured, and were destroyed of the destroyer."

Psalm 34:9 (MSG), "Worship GOD if you want the best; worship opens doors to all his goodness." I believe murmuring/blaming and complaining opens the doors in our lives for the enemy to come in, just like murmuring/blaming and complaining kept the children of Israel from the promises and blessings of God. We, too, can miss out on God's promises and blessings when we murmur and complain. When we complain, we are praising (glorifying) the problem consequently glorying the author of the problem. But I like to be like King David, "A man after God's heart," who always talked about waiting or trusting in the Lord. David talked about his problems in the Psalms but always turned it into praise. Psalm 42:5 reads, "Why art thou cast down, O my soul? And why art thou disquieted in me? Hope [positive expectations] thou in God: for I shall yet praise him." Or consider Job, who said, "Though he slay me, yet will I trust in him" (Job 13:15). <u>Complaining or murmuring about our situation is the polar opposite of trusting God</u>. David said, "It is good for me that I have been afflicted" (Psalms. 119:71). <u>I believe God's Kingdom operates primarily in love according to Galatians 5:6 which states that faith works by love</u>. <u>Worship is expressing our love toward God</u>! When we worship we are operating in God's Kingdom. Satan's kingdom operates under hate and fear. When we hate or operate in fear we also complain. When we complain we are operating under Satan's kingdom.

I do not mean that we cannot share our hurts and problems with other Christian brothers and sisters, for Galatians 6:2 says, "Bear ye one another's burdens, and so fulfill the law of Christ." No, what I'm talking about is complaining about the problem and giving power to that problem, thereby nullifying the power of God. Our words are seeds that will grow in our hearts!

As I said earlier; I see a very close similarity between Christians today and the children of Israel who didn't get into the Promised Land. The children of Israel complained and didn't get into the Promised Land. And Christians today don't receive God's promises because they complain.

The children of Israel blamed and didn't get into the Promised Land. And Christians today don't receive God's promises because they blame. Our faith is activated (or empowered) by what we say and do. Our doubt is also activated (or empowered) by what we say and do.

BLAMING

Don't let your frustrations dictate your BEHAVIOR! One's behavior, many times, becomes one's identity. They blame others for the troubles they create. When people blame others, they make themselves victims. I personally know of young people who are so angry and distrustful (chips on their shoulders) toward their teachers that they don't learn the things they need to go to the next level.

I personally know of people who are continuously in and out of jail or prison because of the chips on their shoulders, but they always have someone to blame for their incarceration. <u>When you blame someone, you give him or her the power over your life</u>! When we blame people, we make them responsible for our actions and behaviors. You can't be the boss if you can't be responsible; you can't be responsible if you blame others! Making a decision to forgive is not blaming the person for the hurts but taking responsibility for how you feel and moving on.

If I blame my sister for not teaching me to tie my shoe and choose to remain unknowledgeable in that area, my sister indirectly controls what goes on my feet. If I blame my brother for not teaching me to drive and I choose to not learn another way, then because I don't know how to drive, he indirectly controls where I go. If I blame my mother for not teaching me to read, she indirectly controls what I can learn. If I blame my father for not teaching me how to treat a woman, he indirectly controls how I treat my wife. (*If I blame someone for what I can or can't do, I give him or her the power over what I can and can't do). Growing up in the 60s and 70s in a poor neighborhood I have seen people smarter and hard working not move forward because they blamed the man. They gave away their power to change their situation by giving their power to the man! Even if it is someone's fault you have to take responsibility for where you are in life to change where you are in life!*

People want the role and respect of the boss but won't take responsibility for the small things that go wrong in life. If a person can't take responsibility for the small things in life, how can he or she take responsibility for the larger things in life? You can't be the boss if you can't be responsible; you can't be responsible if you blame others!

Young men get pissed off or angry because they feel others are pissing on them, but the reality is that they are pissing in the wind! They are their own worst enemies! They can't see how they are hurting themselves, so they blame others. Proverbs 25:21-22 says, "If thine enemy be hungry give him bread to eat; and if thine enemy be thirsty give him water to drink. For thou shalt heap coals of fire upon his head, and the Lord shall reward thee." In working with young people in gangs, I have seen that they create their own enemy. If your enemy is hungry, give him food! They say, "No! He deserves to be hungry!" And if your enemy is thirsty, give him water! They say, "No! He doesn't deserve water to drink." They blame other groups of people for the problems they create. They say they don't deserve mercy.

Some Christians are only nice to get back at others. They want to heap coals of fire upon their heads (as referenced in the previous paragraph). If you are only being nice to others to hurt them, you have resentment in your heart. I remind the reader of several scriptures. The first is in Proverbs 4:23, which reads, "Keep thy heart with all diligence; for out of it are the issues of life." Blaming is saying things to justify your anger.

Job 2:9-10 says, "His wife said to him are you still holding on to your integrity? Curse God and die! He replied, you are talking like a foolish woman. Shall we accept good from God, and not trouble? In all this Job did not sin in what he said" (NIV). So what did Job say while going through his trouble? From the Message Bible Job 2:10, "He said nothing against God." In other words; Job did not blame God. What did Job say? Job praised and worshipped God. Job 13:15 also says, "Though He slay me yet will I trust Him". Job did not blame God. Job only spoke words of faith and trust in God.

Unfortunately, blaming can become a way of life. Some people always make excuses or blame others for failing before they fail. I have had students one-third or one-fourth of the way through one class blame the drama they have to deal with at home for the reason why they are going to fail the class. For most of those students, blaming has become a way of life.

Some students feel unworthy of receiving good things. If you don't think you are worthy of receiving good things, chances are you won't receive them. If you do receive good things and you think you don't deserve them, most likely you will find some way of sabotaging it.

Divorced men and women blame their ex-spouses for their divorces. This may be hard to believe, but I have found hardened criminals blame their victims for their crime. I have heard rapists blame their victims' clothing for causing the rape. Robbers blame their victims' fighting back for the reason they killed them. Gang members blame the deceased rival gang member for killing their fellow gangsters or loved ones. Like racists of old, they say he/she is now a good blank gang member. Gangsters kill people for telling the truth. They call it killing a snitch! Some people blame

God. If a person can justify their sin they will continue in that sin! We all have to control our passions, or our passions will control us! One of the hardest hurts to deal with is guilt and shame of the past.

As a black male counselor, I have experienced counseling people about racism on three different occasions of doing therapy with Caucasian students coming to talk to me about how they felt regarding the unfairness of life. They believed it was minorities, specifically blacks and Hispanics, keeping them from getting good jobs or getting into college. The first two times this happened, I felt like I had to explain the history of racism, realizing that the only reasons why my head is above the sewage of life is because of God and the shoulders I am standing on of the people who have sacrificed their lives so I can have a better life. They seemed to remain bitter and continued to blame. The third time a white student came and talked to me about how he felt about his believed plight in life and his belief that it was because of the blacks and Hispanics, I refocused his thinking on his choices to control his future. I tried to help him realize that by blaming others, he was limiting himself. As long as he had someone to blame, he did not have to take responsibility for his future. We talked about the fact that he could not be successful unless he was responsible. Also, he was not being responsible for himself as long as he was blaming others. I personally believe God wants us to be successful, so the only person that can hold you back is yourself. But we unknowingly hold ourselves back by blaming others.

You can't be the boss if you can't be responsible; you can't be responsible if you blame others! Making a decision to forgive is not blaming the person for the hurts but taking responsibility for how you feel and moving on. People want the <u>role and responsibility</u> of the boss but won't take responsibility for the petty things that go wrong in life. If a person can't take responsibility for the small things in life, how can he or she take responsibility over the larger things in life?

There was a song we sang in church taken from Exodus 14:14, "The Lord shall fight for you, and ye shall hold your peace." The song said, "If I hold my peace and let the Lord fight my battles, Victory! Victory! shall be mine!" We want the victory, but we want to fight our own battles! If we want to win, we need God's help!

When we blame someone for making us feel bad we make ourselves slaves to that person; we have given up the power over our feelings. Most of our decisions are motivated by our feelings, not our thinking or our thoughts about things. We have to take responsibility for our feelings and emotions. It is okay to be sad or grieving but it is a sin to stay in that emotional state. When you blame someone you are really blaming God! It is hard to blame someone, and trust God at the same time! Again we have to trust God! Believe that God will use everything that happens to work for our good. If it is not in faith, it is sin. We walk by faith, not by sight. If we go by what it looks like and what it feels like, we are entering into sin.

CONTENTMENT

I define contentment as being happy with what you have. "But godliness with <u>contentment is great gain</u>", 1Timothy 6:6. Writing and speaking your gratitude list helps you to become happier and more content. One of the most popular scriptures is the 23rd Psalm that starts, "The LORD *is* my shepherd; I shall not want." Why? Because He gives everything I need! In fact, other translations of that scripture read "GOD, my shepherd! I don't need a thing." Message Bible, "The LORD is my shepherd. I am never in need." God's Word, "The LORD is my shepherd; there is nothing I lack." Holman Christian Standard Bible, "The LORD is my shepherd, I lack nothing" New International Version, to name a few translations.

Earlier we talked about sowing and reaping and that our lives tend to go in the direction we focus. When we sow contentment (being happy with what we have) we reap more things to be happy about. When we focus on being content (being happy with what we have) our life tends to go in the direction that brings more happiness! Thus when we are content we get great gain! I Timothy 6:6 Amplified Bible [And it is, indeed, a source of immense profit, for] godliness accompanied with contentment (that contentment, which is a sense of inward sufficiency) is great *and* abundant gain. We must sow (or broadcast) more of what we are happy about than what we are unhappy about. We must focus on more of what we are happy about than what we are unhappy about. If we believe that the thing we don't have is the thing we need to make us happy we will continue to look to the things we don't have to make us happy! Happiness becomes elusive like trying to catch the wind. When we think we have it, we feel the breeze and realize we don't have it. Forever running after it but never catching it. We develop a mindset of, "I'll be happy when!" I'm not sure where I got this idea, maybe from a childhood sermon I heard, but the idea is that joy is a choice that you make. You can choose to be joyful, however, happiness depends on your circumstances. We think we are chasing after things such as money, houses or jobs, but we are really chasing the feeling that those things give us.

We began to have a mindset of having to have things to make us happy. That is where we somehow need things from the outside to make us feel good on the inside. I would be happy if my spouse treated me better. I would be happy if I got a new house or car. The mindset of "I will be happy if" demonstrates a lack of contentment. Again, we must choose to be happy! Contentment. It is the idea of being happy with what you have. I believe we can allow the outside to affect our inside (emotions) or we can allow our inside contentment to affect our outside. Sowing happiness on the inside causes us to reap happiness for our outside. We can help to create an atmosphere of love and peace where blessed people bless people or we can create an atmosphere of disappointment and pain where hurting people hurt people. One exercise is to take a few deep breaths, close your eyes, and imagine yourself at a time in your life when you were the happiest. Think about the feeling of the smile on your face. Focus on the feeling on your cheeks while smiling. Let that feeling spread all over your body. Visualize a time when you were happy. Mark 8:36 expresses, "For what shall it profit a man, if he shall gain the whole world, and lose his own soul?

PROPHECY, PREDICTION ABOUT UNGRATEFUL PEOPLE! *ENTITLEMENT MENTALITY*

I Timothy 3:1-2 (NKJV) states, "But know this, that in the last days perilous times will come: ²⁾ For men will be lovers of themselves, lovers of money, boasters, proud, blasphemers, disobedient to parents, <u>unthankful</u>, unholy." In the New International Version, it says ungrateful instead of unthankful. I'm focusing from that scripture on being unthankful.

Now concerning *Entitlement Mentality*, people feel entitled to things so they don't feel they need to say or feel thankful for anything. People today are becoming more and more inconsiderate. They are unthankful and ungrateful. They don't seem to appreciate anything; as though someone owes them something. I have seen people get things they wanted but get mad that it took so long for them to get it. My wife told me of an old saying of my mother-in-law. She would say when she was growing up, "People are crying with a loaf of bread under their arm." In that they, are crying for food with bread in their hands. The children of Israel had heavenly bread but complained about not having fish, cucumbers, melons, leeks, onions, and garlic (<u>Numbers 11:5</u>). We, too, have everything we need but still complain. II Peter 1:3 Good News Translation, "<u>God's divine power has given us everything we need to live</u> a truly religious life through our knowledge of the one who called us to share in his own glory and goodness. We should be considerate just as it is explained in Philippians 4:5-6 (GW), "Let everyone know how considerate you are. The Lord is near. Never worry about anything. But in every situation let God know what you need in prayers and requests while giving thanks."

People's confessions bring their possessions. Your confessions bring your possessions. I see our words as seeds that we plant: Seeds that produce healthy life-giving fruit; And seeds that are poisonous fruits; Seed that produce praise to God; or seeds that praise the author of confusion. We have a command to, "be fruitful and multiply." Genesis 1:29 and Genesis 9:1 says, "What seeds are you planting?" We multiply what we sow or say!

As a counselor, I have seen life-saving disclosure/debriefing about a past issue that brought the client's freedom. And I have seen people talking about past hurts that reinforced the past hurts. They would angrily talk about the past hurt reinforcing their anger. I have seen small problems become bigger problems by what they continue to say to themselves. They call it, "Getting hyped up!" I have seen others say things to them to get them to say those things to themselves, thereby getting them hyped up! Talking (rehearsing) about the hurtful issue strengthens the hurt feelings about the issue. We begin to trust in what we see and feel more than trusting in God! We can talk about how bad things are but we should not reinforce the negative feelings. II Corinthians 5:7 (KJV), "For we walk by faith, not by sight." When we complain, we are walking by our sight--not faith. I want to reinforce the idea! Complaining glorifies and magnifies the problem thus glorifying the author of that problem. I see many Christians today giving more glory to Satan than they give to God! Hebrews 11:6, "But without faith it is impossible to please Him: for he that cometh to God must believe that he is, and that he is a rewarder of them that diligently seek him" and those that diligently trust Him.

DRUNK IN THE SPIRIT

Ephesians 5:18-20 says, "And be not drunk with wine, wherein is excess; but be filled with the Spirit;[19] Speaking to yourselves in psalms and hymns and spiritual songs, singing and making melody in your heart to the Lord. "Don't get drunk on wine, which leads to wild living. Instead, be filled with the Spirit <u>by</u> reciting psalms, hymns, and spiritual songs for your own good. Sing and make music to the Lord with your hearts. [20] Always thank God the Father for everything in the name of our Lord Jesus Christ. **Revelation 12:11** And they overcame him by the blood of the Lamb, and by the word of their testimony; and they loved not their lives unto the death. <u>We overcome by what we say!</u> Some people deal with stress by drinking or getting drunk or getting high. God's Word Translation says, "Instead, be filled with the Spirit [19] <u>by</u> reciting psalms, hymns, and spiritual songs (GW)."

We can worship God to the point where we become intoxicated or baptized or immersed in the Spirit. Romans 15:13 (NIV) says, "May the God of hope fill you with all joy and peace as you trust in him, so that <u>you may overflow</u> with hope by the power of the Holy

Spirit. If we thought of our lives as a boat and the Holy Spirit as a flowing river; the more of the river gets into the boat the more it will go with the flow of the river. When the boat is submerged under the river (the Holy Spirit) the more the boat (our lives) will yield to the flow of the Spirit. The less we have of the river, the Holy Spirit in our lives (boat) the less we will go with the flow of the river (Holy Spirit). The Holy Spirit is a gentleman. He won't force you to do anything. God will never leave us. In **1 Thessalonians 5:18-19** In everything give thanks: (worship) for this is the will of God in Christ Jesus concerning you. [19)] Quench not the Spirit. We quench the Spirit by not staying in the flow or movement of the Spirit. Again, the Holy Spirit is a gentleman. We have a choice. Psalm 119:171 (NIV) expresses, "May my lips overflow with praise, for you teach me your decrees. Psalm 68:3 (GW) declares, "But let righteous people rejoice. Let them celebrate in God's presence. Let them overflow with joy." In worship, we become intimate, with God. We get closer to God. In intimacy we have a love that casts out fear.

2 Peter 1:3-4 This power was given to us through knowledge of the one who called us by his own glory and integrity.[4] Through his glory and integrity he has given us his promises that are of the highest value. Through these promises you will share in the divine nature because you have escaped the corruption that sinful desires cause in the world (II Peter 1:3-5 GW). Philippians 4:19 (KJV) reads, "But my God shall supply all your need according to his riches in glory by Christ Jesus." In Psalm 26:7 (NIV) it reads, "proclaiming aloud your praise and telling of all your wonderful deeds."

PERCEPTIONS

Many times when we have issues or problems; the problem is not the problem, it is our attitude about the problem or our perceptions about the problem. Many times I have worked with students that have anger control difficulties stemming from an absent father. They say that they can't forgive him because he is a deadbeat dad. I try to change their perception; I explain that many deadbeat dads are really just dead broke dads! They want to be part of their kids' lives but don't want to show up empty handed. They don't want to see their kids without being able to help their kids. If I can get them to see the problem differently, they become more willing to release the pain that induces their anger.

One's perception is one's reality! When we change how we see things in life we change our behavior. When we have a problem our energy level goes down; we are less focused and less determined. But when we see something as a challenge, just the opposite happens. People who are more energized become more focused and more determined.

You can give a smart class and a not so smart class the same test. In the smart class, you tell them this is a hard test. Tell them that you hate giving them this test but just to try. Don't worry if you don't do well because it is so hard. To the not so smart class tell them you are challenging them to see how well they will do on the test. Say I know you are smart but I want to know just how smart you are? In most cases, the not so smart class will do better just because they saw it as a challenge rather than a problem. There are many examples of seeing issues as a challenge verses seeing them as a problem. But there are two that stand out. Some youths try out for little league football. The coach sends in a kid to block a kid that has been playing for a few years. The kid goes in to try to block the experienced player. The experienced player knocks the new player on his backside. The kid comes out crying, throwing his helmet down and saying, "I hate football, I'm never going to play this stupid game again!" The coach sends in another kid. The same thing happens to him. He gets up and tries again. The coach says get lower. The experienced player knocks him on his backside again. He gets up and tries again and the coach says get even lower. The experienced player knocks him on his backside again. The same thing happens over and over. Each time it takes longer for the experienced player to knock him down. The initial outcomes were the same; being knocked down. One stopped but the other kept going because of their perspectives. The first saw it as a problem while the other saw it as a challenge. One's perspective, for the most part, determines one's outcome. In the second example, the same can be said about Joseph the dreamer. We read in Genesis 50:20 (NKJV), "But as for you, you meant evil against me; *but* <u>God meant it for good, in order to bring it about as *it is*</u> <u>this day, to save many people alive</u>." We, too, can take a Godly perspective in life. If we really believe, "we know (perspective) that all things work together for good to them that love God, to them who are the called according to His purpose", Romans 8:28. When we look at things from God's perspective, we move beyond our preconceived ideas about people and things. We learn to trust God regardless.

God wants us to take a Godly perspective! Satan wants us to take a negative perception of life issues. Satan wants us to complain when it rains. God wants us to sell umbrellas. "All things work together for good to them that love God." As an inner-city intervention counselor, I try to help people overcome their challenges by changing their perceptions by words of wisdom.

WORDS OF WISDOM

I use these Words of Wisdom or WOW! to help change perceptions. Your success is in proportion to how well you take correction. *"People who reject correction are rejecting success!"*

Think for a moment. Rappers like Snoop Dog or 50 Cent and others did not come off the streets knowing everything about music and the music industry. Just looking at their hard angry persona, one may assume that they just made it happen. No! They had to <u>listen</u> to the people who knew what to do and how to do it! If your life is stuck and going nowhere don't get mad at the world and the people around you. Just <u>listen</u> to the people who know what to do and how to do it! Just remember, if you reject the correction you are rejecting your success! *Love is stronger than hate!*

Young people believe they have more power by anger and hate. I reminded them that there were two camps of thought in winning the civil rights battle. There was one camp of violence. The other camp was of nonviolence. One camp believed that if someone hit you, that you would hit them back. If they kill one of you then you kill one of them. If they used force to keep you out, then you used force to make your way in. The other way was of love and nonviolence. The two ways were the natural ways of retaliation/violence, and the spiritual way of nonviolence, love, and forgiveness. Civil rights were won spiritually through love, forgiveness and a lot of prayer! I believe that we would not have the civil rights we have today if the fight had been fought in the natural arena with guns and knives. In the battles in your life are you fighting in the natural or spiritual realm? Are you using hate or love? Love is stronger than hate! **Galatians 5:6 "...** but faith which work by love."

Respect will get you further and open more doors than money.

In the late 80s or 90s, we had one of the richest men in America to run for president, H. Ross Perot. Many people became worried that someone so rich could upset our democratic process by using more personal money for campaigning than others. Many thought that he would spend enough money to buy the presidency. He did not get close to becoming president because people did not respect him. Many years later, we had, for the first time, a black man as president. Think for a moment. Do you think people would have voted for him if they did not respect him? Respect can get you a position that money can't get you! Think for a moment if you had a business and to expand your business you have to promote one of two workers that have been working for you the longest. One worker knows more about your business, but is rude and disrespectful. Your customers and other workers complain about him. You know what they are saying is true because he is disrespectful to you as well. The second worker knows a lot, but doesn't know as much about the business, but is respectful. Your customers, other workers, and the rude disrespectful worker all trust him because of his respectful attitude. The business person that wants to make more money will promote the respectful one. Respect will take you further than knowledge!

Example of Respect

Barack Obama never responded to negative disrespectful comments. he seemed to be above the negative talk and would not stoop to the lower level of negative people. I believe Obama respected himself so much that he would not allow others disrespect to lower his respect for himself.

The more you respect yourself the more you can respect others. The less you respect yourself, the less you can respect others. If someone disrespects you, it doesn't weaken your respect for yourself! No one can take away your self-respect; it can only be given away. The more you respect yourself, the harder it is for others to disrespect you. The less you respect yourself, the easier it is for others to disrespect you.

If someone called you a h.o.e. or a punk, you can do one of two things. You can prove them right or prove them wrong? By getting angry and arguing or fighting them you are actually proving them right! But by ignoring them you are proving them wrong! Wisdom is knowing when to keep your mouth closed.

Respect will get you further and open more doors than money.

I know many people that feel like they are held back because of the color of their skin or their last name. The reality is that they are held back because of their disrespectful attitude. If they only showed a tenth of the disrespectful attitude at work as they did around me, I would understand why they are not promoted. If you had a business and your customers complained about their disrespectful attitude, would you promote them? A lot of times people say that's just my personality! Is your attitude making money for the company or losing money?

Responsibility comes before success

Many young people think that one can be successful without being responsible. The reality is if someone gave you a successful business and you didn't do the responsible things to keep the business going, irresponsibility would eventually destroy the business. Look around. The most successful people are the most responsible people. The least responsible people are the least successful. Here's a nugget of wisdom: "Hard work always pays off!"

The biggest influence on your decisions are the people you hang around
When you hang around people who make good decisions, chances are you will make good decisions. But the opposite is true if you hang around people who make bad decisions their bad decisions will influence your bad decisions. You become like the person(s) you spend time with. The most important decisions are influenced by and based on who you spend time with. When you spend time with God and Godly people you become Godly. The opposite is true! The more you spend time with evil or hateful people the more evil or hateful you become!

You have to control the inside before you can control the outside
Think for a moment whether a person can become successful without being able to work through or overcome frustrations. The more you control your inside (emotions) the more you can control your outside (future) life. You have to control the inside of your life before you can control the outside of life! No one can stop you from becoming successful but yourself! The more successful you are in controlling your emotions (or inside) the more you can overcome the challenges of life. Most of our decisions and especially the bad ones are motivated by how we feel; not by what we are thinking! Whether you become rich and famous or poor living on the streets or in prison is based on one thing--the decisions you make! In fact, if someone gave you a successful business but all that you did in the business was make bad decisions (based on negative feelings), your business would soon go bankrupt. It rains on the just and unjust. Also, bad things happen to good people. The people that do not allow the bad things that happen to influence them to make bad decisions have a better chance of controlling and managing their lives. There is a quote from an unknown author that said, "How many people go through life only to find at the end that they could have had it all?" They could have had more

time, more money, more health and more good things instead of so much struggle, stress, and strife. There is an easier way. I believe the easier way is controlling your emotions or feelings!

The difference in successful people and failures are the mistakes they make

A wise man told me, "successful people make more mistakes, but make different mistakes. The people who are failures keep making the same or similar mistakes. When you don't learn from a mistake you will keep making it!" When I first heard this, I did not believe it or understand it. As I thought about it in my life and the lives of people I knew, I realized it was true. I know a person who, in his forties, was making the same mistakes we were making in middle school. In middle school, if he had teachers that told him to do something that he didn't like he would curse them out! In his forties, if his bosses told him to do something he didn't like he would curse them out! He would call me and say, "I can't stand these white folk!" They are putting me down because my skin is brown! They are always trying to tell me what to do! I would say, "They are your bosses. It is their job to tell you what to do!" He didn't learn from his mistakes! I know of people who are always in and out of jail or prison. They didn't learn from their mistakes. It is true that when you make mistakes and get a felony record, it is harder to make good decisions. It may be harder to find a job or a place to live. "But hard doesn't mean impossible!" I know of people who could not find jobs who then went back to illegal things to make money. But I also know of people with felonies, who could only get jobs at a car wash. They started their own car detailing businesses. And I know of others who could not find jobs but started their own lawn care businesses. They learned from their mistakes! The question you have to ask yourself is, "Am I learning from my mistakes?"

ARE YOU POISONING YOURSELF?

Matthews 15:11 says, "Not that which goeth into the mouth defileth (poisons) a man; but that which cometh out of the mouth, this defileth (poisons) a man. Young people listen to music that calls women the "B" word or the "WH" word. When they repeat the words, they poison themselves. Psalm 109:17 (KJV) tells us, "As he loved cursing, so let it come unto him: as he delighted not in blessing, so let it be far from him. And from the Amplified Bible, he also loved cursing, and it came [back] to him; He did not delight in blessing, so it was far from him." We can sing or repeat positive worship songs or negative worldly songs. Con artist tells us the easiest person to fool is the person that thinks he can't be fooled. In that, the person that thinks he can be fooled is more on guard. It is also true that the people that think music has no influence on them is less on guard for the negative influence of that music. **1 Corinthians 15:33 (AMP)** Do not be so deceived *and* misled! Evil companionships (communion, associations) corrupt *and* deprave good manners *and* morals *and* character. Do not be deceived we are influenced (poisoned) by the people we hang around and by what we see and listen to! I believe we have so many murders because we have so many songs using the "N" word which dehumanizes people by making them less than human, thus making it OK to kill them! Songs that use the "B" word dehumanize women equating them to female dogs. **Proverbs 15:4 states** "A wholesome tongue *is* a tree of life: but perverseness therein *is* a breach in the spirit. The tree of life represents the power to give life. Wholesome words give life; negative words poison or destroy life! I encourage my clients to speak positive affirmations (saying positive things to themselves about themselves) to combat negative thoughts and feelings. I also encourage them to set up and look up. There is neuroscience behind looking up or elevating your eyes to elevate your emotions. That is why I believe David said in **Psalm 121:1,** I will lift up mine eyes unto the hills, from whence cometh my help. Also **Psalm 5:3** states, "My voice shalt thou hear in the morning, O LORD; in the morning will I direct *my prayer* unto thee and will look up."

CONCLUSION

Worshiping God is putting God first. In Genesis 4:3-4 it explains, "And <u>in process of time it came to pass, that Cain brought of the fruit of the ground an offering</u> (not first fruits) unto the LORD. 4) And Abel, he also brought of the <u>firstlings of his flock</u> and of the fat thereof. And the LORD had respect unto Abel and to his offering." We bring sacrifices of praise. We put God first in everything in life! We show that God is first by worshiping Him. In the last days, we should be thankful and worship God more!

Prophecy about the day we live in. Reading in II Timothy 3:1-2 we find, "This know also, that in the last days perilous times shall come. 2) For men shall be lovers of their own selves, covetous, boasters, proud, blasphemers, disobedient to parents, <u>unthankful</u>, unholy." Also in Romans 1:21 (KJV) it states, "Because that, when they knew God, they glorified *him* not as God, neither were thankful; but became vain in their imaginations, and their foolish heart was darkened." The Amplified Bible says it this way, "Because when they knew *and* recognized Him as God, they did not honor *and* glorify Him as God or give Him thanks. But instead, they became futile *and* godless in their thinking [with vain imaginings, foolish reasoning, and stupid speculations] and their senseless minds were darkened." We see more and more people today that are lovers of themselves (selfish) desiring wealth, proud and disobedient to parents and authorities. But we overlook people's lack of thankfulness. The Bible is clear. People's hearts become darkened because of the lack of worship and thankfulness. People begin to reason and speculate why good things happen. They rob God, by not giving Him the glory for the things He does for us! We must remember, all the glory belongs to God.

APPENDIX

Gratitude List
Begin on today's date. Write down and say out loud the people places and things for which you are grateful. Also write any notes about the things you're thankful for including:

1. An accomplishment of which you are proud.
2. The first thing to come to mind for which you are grateful.
3. Something you are grateful for today. It can be large or small.

January 1
I am grateful for
1. _____
2. _____
3. _____

Notes

_____
_____
_____

January 3
I am grateful for
1. _____
2. _____
3. _____

Notes

_____
_____
_____

January 2
I am grateful for
1. _____
2. _____
3. _____

Notes

_____
_____
_____

January 4
I am grateful for
1. _____
2. _____
3. _____

Notes

_____
_____
_____

January 5
I am grateful for
1. _____
2. _____
3. _____

Notes
_____
_____
_____
_____

January 7
I am grateful for
1. _____
2. _____
3. _____

Notes
_____
_____
_____
_____

January 6
I am grateful for
1. _____
2. _____
3. _____

Notes
_____
_____
_____
_____

January 8
I am grateful for
1. _____
2. _____
3. _____

Notes
_____
_____
_____
_____

January 9
I am grateful for
1. _____
2. _____
3. _____
Notes
_____
_____
_____
_____

January 11
I am grateful for
1. _____
2. _____
3. _____
Notes
_____
_____
_____
_____

January 10
I am grateful for
1. _____
2. _____
3. _____
Notes
_____
_____
_____
_____

January 12
I am grateful for
1. _____
2. _____
3. _____
Notes
_____
_____
_____
_____

January 13
I am grateful for
1. _____
2. _____
3. _____
Notes
_____
_____
_____
_____

January 15
I am grateful for
1. _____
2. _____
3. _____
Notes
_____
_____
_____
_____

January 14
I am grateful for
1. _____
2. _____
3. _____
Notes
_____
_____
_____
_____

January 16
I am grateful for
1. _____
2. _____
3. _____
Notes
_____
_____
_____
_____

January 17
I am grateful for
1. _____

2. _____

3. _____

Notes
_____
_____
_____
_____

January 19
I am grateful for
1. _____

2. _____

3. _____

Notes
_____
_____
_____
_____

January 18
I am grateful for
1. _____

2. _____

3. _____

Notes
_____
_____
_____
_____

January 20
I am grateful for
1. _____

2. _____

3. _____

Notes
_____
_____
_____
_____

January 21
I am grateful for
1. _____
2. _____
3. _____

Notes
_____
_____
_____
_____

January 22
I am grateful for
1. _____
2. _____
3. _____

Notes
_____
_____
_____
_____

January 23
I am grateful for
1. _____
2. _____
3. _____

Notes
_____
_____
_____
_____

January 24
I am grateful for
1. _____
2. _____
3. _____

Notes
_____
_____
_____
_____

January 25
I am grateful for
1. _____
2. _____
3. _____

Notes

January 27
I am grateful for
1. _____
2. _____
3. _____

Notes

January 26
I am grateful for
1. _____
2. _____
3. _____

Notes

January 28
I am grateful for
1. _____
2. _____
3. _____

Notes

January 29
I am grateful for
1. _____
2. _____
3. _____

Notes
_____
_____
_____
_____

January 31
I am grateful for
1. _____
2. _____
3. _____

Notes
_____
_____
_____
_____

January 30
I am grateful for
1. _____
2. _____
3. _____

Notes
_____
_____
_____
_____

February 1
I am grateful for
1. _____
2. _____
3. _____

Notes
_____
_____
_____
_____

February 2
I am grateful for
1. _____
2. _____
3. _____

Notes
_____
_____
_____
_____

February 4
I am grateful for
1. _____
2. _____
3. _____

Notes
_____
_____
_____
_____

February 3
I am grateful for
1. _____
2. _____
3. _____

Notes
_____
_____
_____
_____

February 5
I am grateful for
1. _____
2. _____
3. _____

Notes
_____
_____
_____
_____

February 6
I am grateful for
1. _____

2. _____

3. _____

Notes

February 8
I am grateful for
1. _____

2. _____

3. _____

Notes

February 7
I am grateful for
1. _____

2. _____

3. _____

Notes

February 9
I am grateful for
1. _____

2. _____

3. _____

Notes

February 10
I am grateful for
1. _____

2. _____

3. _____

Notes
_____
_____
_____
_____

February 12
I am grateful for
1. _____

2. _____

3. _____

Notes
_____
_____
_____
_____

February 11
I am grateful for
1. _____

2. _____

3. _____

Notes
_____
_____
_____
_____

February 13
I am grateful for
1. _____

2. _____

3. _____

Notes
_____
_____
_____
_____

February 14
I am grateful for
1. _____
2. _____
3. _____

Notes

February 16
I am grateful for
1. _____
2. _____
3. _____

Notes

February 15
I am grateful for
1. _____
2. _____
3. _____

Notes

February 17
I am grateful for
1. _____
2. _____
3. _____

Notes

February 18
I am grateful for
1. _____

2. _____

3. _____

Notes

_____
_____
_____
_____

February 20
I am grateful for
1. _____

2. _____

3. _____

Notes

_____
_____
_____
_____

February 19
I am grateful for
1. _____

2. _____

3. _____

Notes

_____
_____
_____
_____

February 21
I am grateful for
1. _____

2. _____

3. _____

Notes

_____
_____
_____

February 22
I am grateful for
1. _____
2. _____
3. _____
Notes
_____
_____
_____

February 23
I am grateful for
1. _____
2. _____
3. _____
Notes
_____
_____
_____

February 24
I am grateful for
1. _____
2. _____
3. _____
Notes
_____
_____
_____

February 25
I am grateful for
1. _____
2. _____
3. _____
Notes
_____
_____
_____

February 26
I am grateful for
1. _____

2. _____

3. _____

Notes
_____
_____
_____

February 28
I am grateful for
1. _____

2. _____

3. _____

Notes
_____
_____
_____

February 27
I am grateful for
1. _____

2. _____

3. _____

Notes
_____
_____
_____

February 29 (only on leap year)
I am grateful for
1. _____

2. _____

3. _____

Notes
_____
_____
_____

Attitude of Gratitude True Worship

March 1
I am grateful for
1. _____

2. _____

3. _____

Notes
_____
_____
_____
_____

March 3
I am grateful for
1. _____

2. _____

3. _____

Notes
_____
_____
_____
_____

March 2
I am grateful for
1. _____

2. _____

3. _____

Notes
_____
_____
_____
_____

March 4
I am grateful for
1. _____

2. _____

3. _____

Notes
_____
_____
_____
_____

March 5
I am grateful for
1. _____

2. _____

3. _____

Notes

March 7
I am grateful for
1. _____

2. _____

3. _____

Notes

March 6
I am grateful for
1. _____

2. _____

3. _____

Notes

March 8
I am grateful for
1. _____

2. _____

3. _____

Notes

March 9
I am grateful for
1. _____
2. _____
3. _____

Notes

March 11
I am grateful for
1. _____
2. _____
3. _____

Notes

March 10
I am grateful for
1. _____
2. _____
3. _____

Notes

March 12
I am grateful for
1. _____
2. _____
3. _____

Notes

March 13
I am grateful for
1. _____
2. _____
3. _____
Notes

March 14
I am grateful for
1. _____
2. _____
3. _____
Notes

March 15
I am grateful for
1. _____
2. _____
3. _____
Notes

March 16
I am grateful for
1. _____
2. _____
3. _____
Notes

Attitude of Gratitude True Worship

March 17
I am grateful for
1. _____
2. _____
3. _____

Notes

March 18
I am grateful for
1. _____
2. _____
3. _____

Notes

March 19
I am grateful for
1. _____
2. _____
3. _____

Notes

March 20
I am grateful for
1. _____
2. _____
3. _____

Notes

March 21
I am grateful for
1. _____
2. _____
3. _____
Notes
_____
_____
_____
_____

March 23
I am grateful for
1. _____
2. _____
3. _____
Notes
_____
_____
_____
_____

March 22
I am grateful for
1. _____
2. _____
3. _____
Notes
_____
_____
_____
_____

March 24
I am grateful for
1. _____
2. _____
3. _____
Notes
_____
_____
_____
_____

March 25
I am grateful for
1. _____
2. _____
3. _____

Notes
_____
_____
_____
_____

March 26
I am grateful for
1. _____
2. _____
3. _____

Notes
_____
_____
_____
_____

March 27
I am grateful for
1. _____
2. _____
3. _____

Notes
_____
_____
_____
_____

March 28
I am grateful for
1. _____
2. _____
3. _____

Notes
_____
_____
_____
_____

March 29
I am grateful for
1. _____
2. _____
3. _____
Notes
_____
_____
_____
_____

March 31
I am grateful for
1. _____
2. _____
3. _____
Notes
_____
_____
_____
_____

March 30
I am grateful for
1. _____
2. _____
3. _____
Notes
_____
_____
_____
_____

April 1
I am grateful for
1. _____
2. _____
3. _____
Notes
_____
_____
_____
_____

April 2
I am grateful for
1. _____
2. _____
3. _____
Notes
_____
_____
_____
_____

April 4
I am grateful for
1. _____
2. _____
3. _____
Notes
_____
_____
_____
_____

April 3
I am grateful for
1. _____
2. _____
3. _____
Notes
_____
_____
_____
_____

April 5
I am grateful for
1. _____
2. _____
3. _____
Notes
_____
_____
_____
_____

April 6
I am grateful for
1. _____
2. _____
3. _____
Notes
_____
_____
_____
_____

April 8
I am grateful for
1. _____
2. _____
3. _____
Notes
_____
_____
_____
_____

April 7
I am grateful for
1. _____
2. _____
3. _____
Notes
_____
_____
_____
_____

April 9
I am grateful for
1. _____
2. _____
3. _____
Notes
_____
_____
_____
_____

April 10
I am grateful for
1. _____

2. _____

3. _____

Notes

April 12
I am grateful for
1. _____

2. _____

3. _____

Notes

April 11
I am grateful for
1. _____

2. _____

3. _____

Notes

April 13
I am grateful for
1. _____

2. _____

3. _____

Notes

April 14
I am grateful for
1. _____
2. _____
3. _____
Notes

April 16
I am grateful for
1. _____
2. _____
3. _____
Notes

April 15
I am grateful for
1. _____
2. _____
3. _____
Notes

April 17
I am grateful for
1. _____
2. _____
3. _____
Notes

April 18
I am grateful for
1. _____

2. _____

3. _____

Notes

April 20
I am grateful for
1. _____

2. _____

3. _____

Notes

April 19
I am grateful for
1. _____

2. _____

3. _____

Notes

April 21
I am grateful for
1. _____

2. _____

3. _____

Notes

April 22
I am grateful for
1. _____
2. _____
3. _____
Notes

April 24
I am grateful for
1. _____
2. _____
3. _____
Notes

April 23
I am grateful for
1. _____
2. _____
3. _____
Notes

April 25
I am grateful for
1. _____
2. _____
3. _____
Notes

April 26
I am grateful for
1. _____
2. _____
3. _____

Notes
_____
_____
_____
_____

April 28
I am grateful for
1. _____
2. _____
3. _____

Notes
_____
_____
_____
_____

April 27
I am grateful for
1. _____
2. _____
3. _____

Notes
_____
_____
_____
_____

April 29
I am grateful for
1. _____
2. _____
3. _____

Notes
_____
_____
_____
_____

April 30
I am grateful for
1. _____
2. _____
3. _____
Notes

May 1
I am grateful for
1. _____
2. _____
3. _____
Notes

May 1
I am grateful for
1. _____
2. _____
3. _____
Notes

May 2
I am grateful for
1. _____
2. _____
3. _____
Notes

May 3
I am grateful for
1. _____
2. _____
3. _____

Notes

May 5
I am grateful for
1. _____
2. _____
3. _____

Notes

May 4
I am grateful for
1. _____
2. _____
3. _____

Notes

May 6
I am grateful for
1. _____
2. _____
3. _____

Notes

May 7
I am grateful for
1. _____
2. _____
3. _____
Notes

May 8
I am grateful for
1. _____
2. _____
3. _____
Notes

May 9
I am grateful for
1. _____
2. _____
3. _____
Notes

May 10
I am grateful for
1. _____
2. _____
3. _____
Notes

May 11
I am grateful for
1. _____
2. _____
3. _____

Notes
_____
_____
_____
_____

May 12
I am grateful for
1. _____
2. _____
3. _____

Notes
_____
_____
_____
_____

May 13
I am grateful for
1. _____
2. _____
3. _____

Notes
_____
_____
_____
_____

May 14
I am grateful for
1. _____
2. _____
3. _____

Notes
_____
_____
_____
_____

May 15
I am grateful for
1. _____
2. _____
3. _____
Notes
_____
_____
_____
_____

May 17
I am grateful for
1. _____
2. _____
3. _____
Notes
_____
_____
_____
_____

May 16
I am grateful for
1. _____
2. _____
3. _____
Notes
_____
_____
_____
_____

May 18
I am grateful for
1. _____
2. _____
3. _____
Notes
_____
_____
_____
_____

May 19
I am grateful for
1. _____
2. _____
3. _____

Notes

May 20
I am grateful for
1. _____
2. _____
3. _____

Notes

May 21
I am grateful for
1. _____
2. _____
3. _____

Notes

May 22
I am grateful for
1. _____
2. _____
3. _____

Notes

May 23
I am grateful for
1. _____

2. _____

3. _____

Notes

May 25
I am grateful for
1. _____

2. _____

3. _____

Notes

May 24
I am grateful for
1. _____

2. _____

3. _____

Notes

May 26
I am grateful for
1. _____

2. _____

3. _____

Notes

May 27
I am grateful for
1. _____
2. _____
3. _____

Notes
_____
_____
_____
_____

May 29
I am grateful for
1. _____
2. _____
3. _____

Notes
_____
_____
_____
_____

May 28
I am grateful for
1. _____
2. _____
3. _____

Notes
_____
_____
_____
_____

May 30
I am grateful for
1. _____
2. _____
3. _____

Notes
_____
_____
_____
_____

May 31
I am grateful for
1. _____
2. _____
3. _____

Notes
_____
_____
_____
_____

June 2
I am grateful for
1. _____
2. _____
3. _____

Notes
_____
_____
_____
_____

June 1
I am grateful for
1. _____
2. _____
3. _____

Notes
_____
_____
_____
_____

June 3
I am grateful for
1. _____
2. _____
3. _____

Notes
_____
_____
_____
_____

June 4
I am grateful for
1. _____
2. _____
3. _____

Notes
_____
_____
_____
_____

June 6
I am grateful for
1. _____
2. _____
3. _____

Notes
_____
_____
_____
_____

June 5
I am grateful for
1. _____
2. _____
3. _____

Notes
_____
_____
_____
_____

June 7
I am grateful for
1. _____
2. _____
3. _____

Notes
_____
_____
_____
_____

June 8
I am grateful for
1. _____
2. _____
3. _____

Notes
_____
_____
_____

June 9
I am grateful for
1. _____
2. _____
3. _____

Notes
_____
_____
_____

June 10
I am grateful for
1. _____
2. _____
3. _____

Notes
_____
_____
_____

June 11
I am grateful for
1. _____
2. _____
3. _____

Notes
_____
_____
_____

June 12
I am grateful for
1. _____
2. _____
3. _____

Notes
_____
_____
_____
_____

June 13
I am grateful for
1. _____
2. _____
3. _____

Notes
_____
_____
_____
_____

June 14
I am grateful for
1. _____
2. _____
3. _____

Notes
_____
_____
_____
_____

June 15
I am grateful for
1. _____
2. _____
3. _____

Notes
_____
_____
_____
_____

June 16
I am grateful for
1. _____
2. _____
3. _____

Notes
_____
_____
_____
_____

June 18
I am grateful for
1. _____
2. _____
3. _____

Notes
_____
_____
_____
_____

June 17
I am grateful for
1. _____
2. _____
3. _____

Notes
_____
_____
_____
_____

June 19
I am grateful for
1. _____
2. _____
3. _____

Notes
_____
_____
_____

June 20
I am grateful for
1. _____
2. _____
3. _____

Notes
_____
_____
_____
_____

June 22
I am grateful for
1. _____
2. _____
3. _____

Notes
_____
_____
_____
_____

June 21
I am grateful for
1. _____
2. _____
3. _____

Notes
_____
_____
_____
_____

June 23
I am grateful for
1. _____
2. _____
3. _____

Notes
_____
_____
_____
_____

June 24
I am grateful for
1. _____
2. _____
3. _____

Notes

June 25
I am grateful for
1. _____
2. _____
3. _____

Notes

June 26
I am grateful for
1. _____
2. _____
3. _____

Notes

June 27
I am grateful for
1. _____
2. _____
3. _____

Notes

June 28
I am grateful for
1. _____
2. _____
3. _____

Notes
_____
_____
_____
_____

June 30
I am grateful for
1. _____
2. _____
3. _____

Notes
_____
_____
_____
_____

June 29
I am grateful for
1. _____
2. _____
3. _____

Notes
_____
_____
_____
_____

July 1
I am grateful for
1. _____
2. _____
3. _____

Notes
_____
_____
_____
_____

July 2
I am grateful for
1. _____
2. _____
3. _____

Notes

July 4
I am grateful for
1. _____
2. _____
3. _____

Notes

July 3
I am grateful for
1. _____
2. _____
3. _____

Notes

July 5
I am grateful for
1. _____
2. _____
3. _____

Notes

Attitude of Gratitude True Worship

July 6
I am grateful for
1. _____

2. _____

3. _____

Notes

July 8
I am grateful for
1. _____

2. _____

3. _____

Notes

July 7
I am grateful for
1. _____

2. _____

3. _____

Notes

July 9
I am grateful for
1. _____

2. _____

3. _____

Notes

July 10
I am grateful for
1. _____
2. _____
3. _____

Notes
_____
_____
_____

July 11
I am grateful for
1. _____
2. _____
3. _____

Notes
_____
_____
_____

July 12
I am grateful for
1. _____
2. _____
3. _____

Notes
_____
_____
_____

July 13
I am grateful for
1. _____
2. _____
3. _____

Notes
_____
_____
_____

July 14
I am grateful for
1. _____
2. _____
3. _____

Notes

July 15
I am grateful for
1. _____
2. _____
3. _____

Notes

July 16
I am grateful for
1. _____
2. _____
3. _____

Notes

July 17
I am grateful for
1. _____
2. _____
3. _____

Notes

July 18
I am grateful for
1. _____

2. _____

3. _____

Notes

July 20
I am grateful for
1. _____

2. _____

3. _____

Notes

July 19
I am grateful for
1. _____

2. _____

3. _____

Notes

July 21
I am grateful for
1. _____

2. _____

3. _____

Notes

July 22
I am grateful for
1. _____
2. _____
3. _____

Notes

July 24
I am grateful for
1. _____
2. _____
3. _____

Notes

July 23
I am grateful for
1. _____
2. _____
3. _____

Notes

July 25
I am grateful for
1. _____
2. _____
3. _____

Notes

July 26
I am grateful for
1. _____
2. _____
3. _____

Notes

July 27
I am grateful for
1. _____
2. _____
3. _____

Notes

July 28
I am grateful for
1. _____
2. _____
3. _____

Notes

July 29
I am grateful for
1. _____
2. _____
3. _____

Notes

July 30
I am grateful for
1. _____
2. _____
3. _____

Notes
_____
_____
_____
_____

August 1
I am grateful for
1. _____
2. _____
3. _____

Notes
_____
_____
_____
_____

August 2
I am grateful for
1. _____
2. _____
3. _____

Notes
_____
_____
_____
_____

August 3
I am grateful for
1. _____
2. _____
3. _____

Notes
_____
_____
_____
_____

August 4
I am grateful for
1. _____

2. _____

3. _____

Notes
_____
_____
_____
_____

August 6
I am grateful for
1. _____

2. _____

3. _____

Notes
_____
_____
_____
_____

August 5
I am grateful for
1. _____

2. _____

3. _____

Notes
_____
_____
_____
_____

August 7
I am grateful for
1. _____

2. _____

3. _____

Notes
_____
_____
_____
_____

Attitude of Gratitude True Worship

August 8
I am grateful for
1. _____
2. _____
3. _____

Notes
_____
_____
_____
_____

August 10
I am grateful for
1. _____
2. _____
3. _____

Notes
_____
_____
_____
_____

August 9
I am grateful for
1. _____
2. _____
3. _____

Notes
_____
_____
_____
_____

August 11
I am grateful for
1. _____
2. _____
3. _____

Notes
_____
_____
_____
_____

August 12
I am grateful for
1. _____

2. _____

3. _____

Notes
_____
_____
_____
_____

August 13
I am grateful for
1. _____

2. _____

3. _____

Notes
_____
_____
_____
_____

August 14
I am grateful for
1. _____

2. _____

3. _____

Notes
_____
_____
_____
_____

August 15
I am grateful for
1. _____

2. _____

3. _____

Notes
_____
_____
_____
_____

August 16
I am grateful for
1. _____
2. _____
3. _____

Notes

August 17
I am grateful for
1. _____
2. _____
3. _____

Notes

August 18
I am grateful for
1. _____
2. _____
3. _____

Notes

August 19
I am grateful for
1. _____
2. _____
3. _____

Notes

August 20
I am grateful for
1. _____
2. _____
3. _____
Notes
_____
_____
_____
_____

August 21
I am grateful for
1. _____
2. _____
3. _____
Notes
_____
_____
_____
_____

August 22
I am grateful for
1. _____
2. _____
3. _____
Notes
_____
_____
_____
_____

August 23
I am grateful for
1. _____
2. _____
3. _____
Notes
_____
_____
_____
_____

August 24
I am grateful for
1. _____
2. _____
3. _____

Notes
_____
_____
_____
_____

August 26
I am grateful for
1. _____
2. _____
3. _____

Notes
_____
_____
_____
_____

August 25
I am grateful for
1. _____
2. _____
3. _____

Notes
_____
_____
_____
_____

August 27
I am grateful for
1. _____
2. _____
3. _____

Notes
_____
_____
_____
_____

August 28
I am grateful for
1. _____

2. _____

3. _____

Notes

August 30
I am grateful for
1. _____

2. _____

3. _____

Notes

August 29
I am grateful for
1. _____

2. _____

3. _____

Notes

September 1
I am grateful for
1. _____

2. _____

3. _____

Notes

Attitude of Gratitude True Worship

September 1
I am grateful for
1. _____
2. _____
3. _____

Notes
_____
_____
_____

September 2
I am grateful for
1. _____
2. _____
3. _____

Notes
_____
_____
_____

September 3
I am grateful for
1. _____
2. _____
3. _____

Notes
_____
_____
_____

September 4
I am grateful for
1. _____
2. _____
3. _____

Notes
_____
_____
_____

September 5
I am grateful for
1. _____

2. _____

3. _____

Notes

September 6
I am grateful for
1. _____

2. _____

3. _____

Notes

September 7
I am grateful for
1. _____

2. _____

3. _____

Notes

September 8
I am grateful for
1. _____

2. _____

3. _____

Notes

Attitude of Gratitude True Worship

September 9
I am grateful for
1. _____
2. _____
3. _____
Notes
_____
_____
_____
_____

September 11
I am grateful for
1. _____
2. _____
3. _____
Notes
_____
_____
_____
_____

September 10
I am grateful for
1. _____
2. _____
3. _____
Notes
_____
_____
_____
_____

September 12
I am grateful for
1. _____
2. _____
3. _____
Notes
_____
_____
_____
_____

September 13
I am grateful for
1. _____
2. _____
3. _____

Notes
_____
_____
_____
_____

September 15
I am grateful for
1. _____
2. _____
3. _____

Notes
_____
_____
_____
_____

September 14
I am grateful for
1. _____
2. _____
3. _____

Notes
_____
_____
_____
_____

September 16
I am grateful for
1. _____
2. _____
3. _____

Notes
_____
_____
_____
_____

Attitude of Gratitude True Worship

September 17
I am grateful for
1. _____
2. _____
3. _____

Notes
_____
_____
_____
_____

September 19
I am grateful for
1. _____
2. _____
3. _____

Notes
_____
_____
_____
_____

September 18
I am grateful for
1. _____
2. _____
3. _____

Notes
_____
_____
_____
_____

September 20
I am grateful for
1. _____
2. _____
3. _____

Notes
_____
_____
_____
_____

September 21
I am grateful for
1. _____

2. _____

3. _____

Notes
_____
_____
_____
_____

September 22
I am grateful for
1. _____

2. _____

3. _____

Notes
_____
_____
_____
_____

September 23
I am grateful for
1. _____

2. _____

3. _____

Notes
_____
_____
_____
_____

September 24
I am grateful for
1. _____

2. _____

3. _____

Notes
_____
_____
_____
_____

Attitude of Gratitude True Worship

September 25
I am grateful for
1. _____
2. _____
3. _____

Notes

September 26
I am grateful for
1. _____
2. _____
3. _____

Notes

September 27
I am grateful for
1. _____
2. _____
3. _____

Notes

September 28
I am grateful for
1. _____
2. _____
3. _____

Notes

September 29
I am grateful for
1. _____

2. _____

3. _____

Notes
_____
_____
_____
_____

September 30
I am grateful for
1. _____

2. _____

3. _____

Notes
_____
_____
_____
_____

October 1
I am grateful for
1. _____

2. _____

3. _____

Notes
_____
_____
_____
_____

October 2
I am grateful for
1. _____

2. _____

3. _____

Notes
_____
_____
_____
_____

October 3
I am grateful for
1. _____
2. _____
3. _____

Notes
_____
_____
_____
_____

October 4
I am grateful for
1. _____
2. _____
3. _____

Notes
_____
_____
_____
_____

October 5
I am grateful for
1. _____
2. _____
3. _____

Notes
_____
_____
_____
_____

October 6
I am grateful for
1. _____
2. _____
3. _____

Notes
_____
_____
_____
_____

October 7
I am grateful for
1. _____

2. _____

3. _____

Notes

_____
_____
_____
_____

October 9
I am grateful for
1. _____

2. _____

3. _____

Notes

_____
_____
_____
_____

October 8
I am grateful for
1. _____

2. _____

3. _____

Notes

_____
_____
_____
_____

October 10
I am grateful for
1. _____

2. _____

3. _____

Notes

_____
_____
_____
_____

October 11
I am grateful for
1. _____
2. _____
3. _____

Notes
_____
_____
_____

October 13
I am grateful for
1. _____
2. _____
3. _____

Notes
_____
_____
_____

October 12
I am grateful for
1. _____
2. _____
3. _____

Notes
_____
_____
_____

October 14
I am grateful for
1. _____
2. _____
3. _____

Notes
_____
_____
_____

October 15
I am grateful for
1. _____
2. _____
3. _____

Notes
_____
_____
_____
_____

October 17
I am grateful for
1. _____
2. _____
3. _____

Notes
_____
_____
_____
_____

October 16
I am grateful for
1. _____
2. _____
3. _____

Notes
_____
_____
_____
_____

October 18
I am grateful for
1. _____
2. _____
3. _____

Notes
_____
_____
_____
_____

Attitude of Gratitude True Worship

October 19
I am grateful for
1. _____
2. _____
3. _____

Notes
_____
_____
_____
_____

October 20
I am grateful for
1. _____
2. _____
3. _____

Notes
_____
_____
_____
_____

October 21
I am grateful for
1. _____
2. _____
3. _____

Notes
_____
_____
_____
_____

October 22
I am grateful for
1. _____
2. _____
3. _____

Notes
_____
_____
_____
_____

October 23
I am grateful for
1. _____

2. _____

3. _____

Notes

October 25
I am grateful for
1. _____

2. _____

3. _____

Notes

October 24
I am grateful for
1. _____

2. _____

3. _____

Notes

October 26
I am grateful for
1. _____

2. _____

3. _____

Notes

Attitude of Gratitude True Worship

October 27
I am grateful for
1. _____
2. _____
3. _____
Notes
_____
_____
_____

October 28
I am grateful for
1. _____
2. _____
3. _____
Notes
_____
_____
_____
_____

October 29
I am grateful for
1. _____
2. _____
3. _____
Notes
_____
_____
_____

October 30
I am grateful for
1. _____
2. _____
3. _____
Notes
_____
_____
_____

October 31
I am grateful for
1. _____
2. _____
3. _____

Notes
_____
_____
_____
_____

November 2
I am grateful for
1. _____
2. _____
3. _____

Notes
_____
_____
_____
_____

November 1
I am grateful for
1. _____
2. _____
3. _____

Notes
_____
_____
_____
_____

November 3
I am grateful for
1. _____
2. _____
3. _____

Notes
_____
_____
_____
_____

November 4
I am grateful for
1. _____
2. _____
3. _____

Notes

November 5
I am grateful for
1. _____
2. _____
3. _____

Notes

November 6
I am grateful for
1. _____
2. _____
3. _____

Notes

November 7
I am grateful for
1. _____
2. _____
3. _____

Notes

November 8
I am grateful for
1. _____

2. _____

3. _____

Notes

November 10
I am grateful for
1. _____

2. _____

3. _____

Notes

November 9
I am grateful for
1. _____

2. _____

3. _____

Notes

November 11
I am grateful for
1. _____

2. _____

3. _____

Notes

November 12
I am grateful for
1. _____
2. _____
3. _____

Notes
_____
_____
_____

November 14
I am grateful for
1. _____
2. _____
3. _____

Notes
_____
_____
_____

November 13
I am grateful for
1. _____
2. _____
3. _____

Notes
_____
_____
_____

November 15
I am grateful for
1. _____
2. _____
3. _____

Notes
_____
_____
_____

November 16
I am grateful for
1. _____
2. _____
3. _____
Notes
_____
_____
_____
_____

November 18
I am grateful for
1. _____
2. _____
3. _____
Notes
_____
_____
_____
_____

November 17
I am grateful for
1. _____
2. _____
3. _____
Notes
_____
_____
_____
_____

November 19
I am grateful for
1. _____
2. _____
3. _____
Notes
_____
_____
_____
_____

Attitude of Gratitude True Worship

November 20
I am grateful for
1. _____
2. _____
3. _____
Notes
_____
_____
_____
_____

November 21
I am grateful for
1. _____
2. _____
3. _____
Notes
_____
_____
_____
_____

November 22
I am grateful for
1. _____
2. _____
3. _____
Notes
_____
_____
_____
_____

November 23
I am grateful for
1. _____
2. _____
3. _____
Notes
_____
_____
_____
_____

November 24
I am grateful for
1. _____
2. _____
3. _____
Notes

November 26
I am grateful for
1. _____
2. _____
3. _____
Notes

November 25
I am grateful for
1. _____
2. _____
3. _____
Notes

November 27
I am grateful for
1. _____
2. _____
3. _____
Notes

Attitude of Gratitude True Worship

November 28
I am grateful for
1. _____

2. _____

3. _____

Notes

_____
_____
_____
_____

November 30
I am grateful for
1. _____

2. _____

3. _____

Notes

_____
_____
_____
_____

November 29
I am grateful for
1. _____

2. _____

3. _____

Notes

_____
_____
_____
_____

December 1
I am grateful for
1. _____

2. _____

3. _____

Notes

_____
_____
_____
_____

December 2
I am grateful for
1. _____
2. _____
3. _____
Notes
_____
_____
_____
_____

December 4
I am grateful for
1. _____
2. _____
3. _____
Notes
_____
_____
_____
_____

December 3
I am grateful for
1. _____
2. _____
3. _____
Notes
_____
_____
_____
_____

December 5
I am grateful for
1. _____
2. _____
3. _____
Notes
_____
_____
_____
_____

December 6
I am grateful for
1. _____
2. _____
3. _____

Notes

December 8
I am grateful for
1. _____
2. _____
3. _____

Notes

December 7
I am grateful for
1. _____
2. _____
3. _____

Notes

December 9
I am grateful for
1. _____
2. _____
3. _____

Notes

December 10
I am grateful for
1. _____
2. _____
3. _____
Notes
_____
_____
_____

December 12
I am grateful for
1. _____
2. _____
3. _____
Notes
_____
_____
_____

December 11
I am grateful for
1. _____
2. _____
3. _____
Notes
_____
_____
_____

December 13
I am grateful for
1. _____
2. _____
3. _____
Notes
_____
_____
_____

Attitude of Gratitude True Worship

December 14
I am grateful for
1. _____

2. _____

3. _____

Notes
_____
_____
_____

December 16
I am grateful for
1. _____

2. _____

3. _____

Notes
_____
_____
_____

December 15
I am grateful for
1. _____

2. _____

3. _____

Notes
_____
_____
_____

December 17
I am grateful for
1. _____

2. _____

3. _____

Notes
_____
_____
_____

December 18
I am grateful for
1. _____
2. _____
3. _____
Notes
_____
_____
_____
_____

December 20
I am grateful for
1. _____
2. _____
3. _____
Notes
_____
_____
_____
_____

December 19
I am grateful for
1. _____
2. _____
3. _____
Notes
_____
_____
_____
_____

December 21
I am grateful for
1. _____
2. _____
3. _____
Notes
_____
_____
_____
_____

Attitude of Gratitude True Worship

December 22
I am grateful for
1. _____
2. _____
3. _____

Notes
_____
_____
_____
_____

December 24
I am grateful for
1. _____
2. _____
3. _____

Notes
_____
_____
_____
_____

December 23
I am grateful for
1. _____
2. _____
3. _____

Notes
_____
_____
_____
_____

December 25
I am grateful for
1. _____
2. _____
3. _____

Notes
_____
_____
_____
_____

December 26
I am grateful for
1. _____
2. _____
3. _____
Notes

December 27
I am grateful for
1. _____
2. _____
3. _____
Notes

December 28
I am grateful for
1. _____
2. _____
3. _____
Notes

December 29
I am grateful for
1. _____
2. _____
3. _____
Notes

December 30
I am grateful for

1. _____

2. _____

3. _____

Notes

_____
_____
_____
_____

December 31
I am grateful for

1. _____

2. _____

3. _____

Notes

_____
_____
_____
_____

www.ingramcontent.com/pod-product-compliance
Lightning Source LLC
Chambersburg PA
CBHW071427160426
43195CB00013B/1832